LAWRENCE OF ARABIA

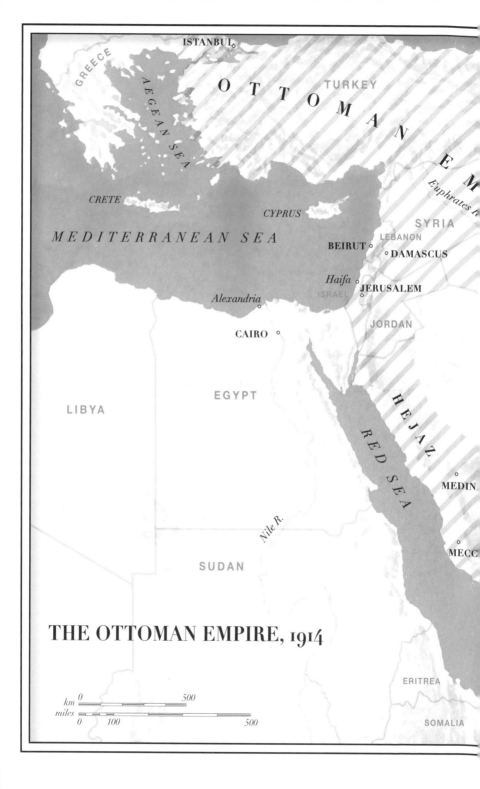

THE OTTOMAN EMPIRE, 1914

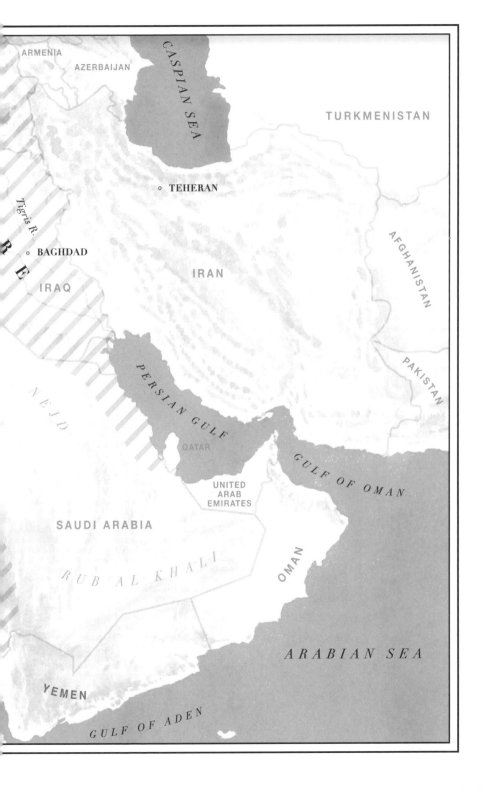

Lawrence of Arabia

LAWRENCE OF ARABIA

ALISTAIR MACLEAN

STERLING PUBLISHING CO., INC.
New York

A FLYING POINT PRESS BOOK

Design: PlutoMedia
Front cover photograph: Corbis
Back cover and frontispiece photograph: Imperial War Museum

Library of Congress Cataloging-in-Publication Data Available

2 4 6 8 10 9 7 5 3 1

Published by Sterling Publishing Co., Inc.
387 Park Avenue South, New York, NY 10016
Original edition published by Random House, Inc.
Copyright © 1962 by Devoran Trustees Limited
New material in this updated edition
Copyright © 2006 by Flying Point Press
Maps copyright © by Richard Thompson, Creative Freelancers, Inc.
Distributed in Canada by Sterling Publishing
c/o Canadian Manda Group, 165 Dufferin Street
Toronto, Ontario, Canada M6K 3H6
Distributed in the United Kingdom by GMC Distribution Services
Castle Place, 166 High Street, Lewes, East Sussex, England BN7 1XU
Distributed in Australia by Capricorn Link (Australia) Pty. Ltd.
P.O. Box 704, Windsor, NSW 2756, Australia

Sterling ISBN-13: 978-1-4027-3613-1
ISBN-10: 1-4027-3613-4

For information about custom editions, special sales, premium and
corporate purchases, please contact Sterling Special Sales
Department at 800-805-5489 or specialsales@sterlingpub.com.

Contents

MAPS

LAWRENCE OF ARABIA

CHAPTER 1

THE LAND OF ARABIA

WHAT IS ARABIA? WHERE IS ARABIA? NEEDLESS questions, some may say. You have only to turn the pages of an atlas and there it is, enclosed on three sides by the Red Sea, the Arabian Sea and the Persian Gulf. To the north it is bounded by Iraq, Jordan and Kuwait. The word "Arabia"—or "Saudi Arabia"—is written large across it.

True, that is Arabia, Arabia as we think of it today, but this story concerns itself not with today but with the early years of last century. In North America, in Great Britain, we think of the boundaries of our countries as being fixed and permanent. This is because in our time, in the time of our grandfathers, perhaps for hundreds of years, they *have* been fixed and permanent. But in Eastern Europe and Asia the boundaries of a nation have frequently changed several times in the span of a single lifetime. So has it been with Arabia, which is not now the same country it was at the time of the First World War.

Could we say, then, that Arabia is the home of the Arabs? It sounds logical enough, but again we come up against difficulties. Great numbers of Arabs live in North Africa, and in this story we are not concerned with what lies to the west of the Red Sea. Besides, there are so many different racial groups of Arabs, gradually shading off into other races, that it is impossible to say definitely who is Arab and who is not.

For our purpose, perhaps the best definition as to what is Arabia is that laid down by the geographers and geologists. They are concerned not with the artificial boundaries drawn by man but with the physical barriers created by nature.

Look at a colored relief map of the Middle East. Follow the great wall of mountain that runs from the Aegean Sea east through Turkey and then southeast into Iran or Persia, as it used to be known. This great mountain barrier is the real frontier, a boundary line drawn by the hand of nature twenty million years ago. All of the great peninsula lying to the south of this we may regard as the real Arabia. Admittedly, this includes not only modern Saudi Arabia but also Iraq, Syria, Jordan, Israel, Lebanon, and several other countries. But no matter, this is the true Arabia.

A vast land is this Arabia, vaster perhaps than many realize. Were this peninsula placed in the heart of North America, it would cover most of the Great Plains from the Allegheny Mountains clear across to the divide of the Rockies. And it would stretch from the Mexican border northward into Canada.

It is a vast land and a hard and cruel one, a land of incredible contrasts. To the north, east and south there lie great limitless stretches of desert. The wasteland of Rub al Khali to the south is about the size of Texas, and its deserts of sand and gravel and rock burn all day under a pitiless white sun. The lone traveler, without camel or water, lost in the baking oven heat of those barren wastes, will have little enough time to bewail his fate before death overtakes him. He will surely die from exhaustion and thirst and madness.

But the lost traveler in Arabia can die from other causes, too. He can freeze to death, buried under the fierce blizzards that sweep down from suddenly darkened skies. These storms blanket the high mountains to the east and north under a deep and impassable cover of snow. It does seem incredible, for it is very difficult to associate the idea of snow with the subtropical Arabian Peninsula. But winter snowfall in the mountains of the Hejaz, in Jordan and Kurdistan, is the rule and not the exception. On Mount Lebanon there is snow all summer.

The climate is not everywhere, of course, so extreme. To the north, the fertile crescent of the Euphrates valley and the Mediterranean coast is just that—a fertile crescent. On the hilly seaward slopes overlooking the Red and Arabian seas the climate is reasonably mild and pleasant. The air in the Nejd, the high plateau in the heart of Saudi Arabia, is dry and bracing and unpleasantly hot only for brief periods in the height of summer.

But those are the exceptions, the relatively mild exceptions in which we find most of the cities and the towns of the Arabian Peninsula. Arabia, as a whole, remains a harsh and bitter land where the first and by far the most important necessity of life is that of simple survival.

It requires a very special type of man to survive those conditions of drought, desert and blazing heat. And the Bedouin, the wandering Arab of the desert, is just that: a very special type of man indeed. And it is with the Bedouin, as distinct from the Arab of the towns and cities, that we shall be chiefly concerned in this story.

No one knows how long the Bedouins have been roaming the deserts of Arabia—certainly since before the dawn of recorded history. The Bedouin is a nomad, a wanderer by necessity, for he lives by his herds of camels, his horse and his sheep. And for those he must have pasture. There are no lush green fields in Arabia such as we know in temperate lands. The pastures are small and thin and parched and quickly grazed, so that the Bedouin must soon move on to other feeding grounds where winter rains have caused grass to grow. And he can use only those pastures where water is to be found.

It is difficult for us to appreciate the hardship of the Bedouin existence. These people have no settled homes, no land and few possessions other than the animals under their care. They must be constantly on the move, burned by the sun, choked by the sandstorms of the desert, always on the alert for an enemy. Hunger and thirst are the daily companions of these nomads of the desert. If a Bedouin's entire food and drink between dawn and sunset consist of a handful of dates and a gourd of brackish water, he thinks himself both fortunate and satisfied. Generations of hardship have made the Bedouin tough; he not only survives all this, he thrives on it.

Even tougher than the Bedouin is the camel itself. For the typical Bedouin the camel is by far the most important thing in life; it is the central act of his existence. Without it, he could not survive. To a great extent, the only money the Bedouin ever earns and the only possessions he can buy come from the sale of camels he has reared.

The single-humped camel is the chief means of transport in the desert. It provides the Bedouin with milk and, when starvation is at hand, with meat. From its hair comes the raw material for clothes; from its skin, the stuff for tents. Its sinews are used for ropes and thongs. The camel, in short, can supply most of the Bedouin's material needs in life.

The camel is also magnificently suited for survival in the desert. Widespread hoofs spread the load of his weight in the soft sand, while thick heavy pads protect the hoofs from the broiling heat of bare rock. Thus the camel can walk unharmed over razor-edged flints that would lay the hoof of another animal open to the bone. More pads on the knees and chest enable it to kneel in comfort. The big flaring nostrils can be completely closed against sandstorms. As further protection, its ears are tiny in the extreme.

Some camels can carry up to 1,000 pounds in weight, although only for brief periods. And nearly any camel can carry a load of 500 pounds for thirty miles a day for five days on end without requiring much—if any—food or water. This is because of a camel's unique gift of storing up food in the form of fat in its single hump. Also, the camel retains large quantities of water for a long time, because it sweats very little. And, to make matters perfect for the Bedouin, the camel can live by eating the otherwise useless needle-pointed spines of the desert thorn bush. No other animal alive can do this.

The Bedouins, like all nomad races, band themselves

into tribes. Each tribe is ruled by a sheik, or emir, who guides them in peace, leads them in war and settles all difficulties between members of the tribe. The Bedouins also owe some allegiance to the king or prince or president in whose land they live. But their own sheik and their own tribe are much more important to them than king and country. What lies beyond their desert horizons is of little interest. Leave the Bedouin his pride and independence, allow him to follow his age-old traditional ways of living—and he can ask no more from life.

In the early years of the last century, all Arabia from the Mediterranean to Persia, from Kurdistan in the north to the Arabian Sea in the south lay under the harsh rule of the Ottoman Empire of the Turks.

Turkey, which at that time was having more than enough trouble with Russia, the Balkans and Italy, would have been much happier had this harsh and brutal rule not been necessary. To keep control of a land the size of the Arabian Peninsula requires much time and trouble. It also requires the spending of a great deal of money. Scores of barracks have to be built throughout the land, and these must be manned by garrisons big enough to quell trouble wherever and whenever it arises.

It would have suited the Turks much better if the Arabs, as fellow Moslems or Mohammedans, had quietly settled down in the role of the inferior partners, meekly obeying and submissively cooperating with their Turkish overlords. Alas for the hopes of the Turks, obedience to and cooperation with a foreign oppressor were two qualities that the Arabs had never learned in all their long history.

Discontent, defiance and open armed rebellion were the order of the day. In Syria, and in what are now Jordan and Iraq—the parts of the Arabian region most directly under the rule of the Turks—many secret societies flourished. These societies organized guerrilla and sabotage bands to attack Turkish occupation troops and installations. The rebel Arabs had apparently forgotten, or were unaware of, how the Turks behaved toward people who opposed them. In the twenty years following 1895, the Turks were said to have massacred, or caused the death of 800,000 Armenians. Some of these Armenians were killed because of their Christian Beliefs; others because they were accused of helping the Russian army fight Turkey.

And now the turn of the Arabs had come. Any captured member of an Arabian secret society or guerrilla band was put to death. Then, in the area where he had been caught, the Turks would seize every man—peaceful peasant or harmless shepherd though he might be—and hang him. If a suspected secret society member belonged to a certain village, the Turks would turn loose their troops and massacre every single man, woman and child in that village.

For every man the Turks lost, the Arabs would lose a hundred. For the northern Arabs the cost of the struggle for freedom became too appallingly high. Soon their resistance to the Turks ceased altogether.

The result was that shortly before the outbreak of World War I all hope of deliverance lay with the Arabs to the south, in the country we now recognize as Saudi Arabia. There the nomadic Bedouin tribes, first-class guerrilla fighters, could vanish at will into the vast depths of the desert, safe from all threat of massacre or retaliation. This was a tremendous advantage in times of war.

Unfortunately the Bedouins possessed an equally great drawback. These Arabs of the south carried their ideals of freedom and independence—not to mention their age-old feuds and suspicions—too far. They would not even unite among themselves. The whole peninsula was divided into a number of larger and smaller kingdoms. There were at least three along the Persian Gulf, two along the Arabian Sea and two in the heart of the country. Then there were numerous smaller areas ruled over by emirs or sheiks who stoutly refused to owe allegiance to anyone. The chances of uniting those far-scattered peoples, each with its own private interests and high degree of distrust of the others, seemed very remote indeed.

But there did seem to be a possibility of uniting a large part of the country under the leadership of one of its two greatest kingdoms. Those were the kingdom of Nejd, in the very heart of Arabia and the kingdom of Hejaz, the land that lay to the west between Nejd and the northern half of the Red Sea.

The hope for a Nejd-based uprising came to nothing. Nejd remained neutral during the war, though she did have a treaty with Great Britain. This left only the Hejaz, the land of the holy cities of Mecca and Medina. The Hejaz was ruled by the Emir Hussein ibn Ali, the Sherif of

Mecca. The title "Sherif" indicated that he was a direct descendant of Mohammed. Hussein, who had been installed by the Turks, had four sons: Ali, Abdullah, Feisal and Zeid.

The third son, Feisal, a born leader and splendid soldier, held the unquestioned devotion and respect of the Bedouin tribes of the Hejaz. He was to become the Arabian man of destiny.

In the autumn of 1914, Britain and France went to war with Germany. Turkey came in on the German side, almost inevitably so, because for many years the friendship and military contact between the Germans and the Turks had been very close. German officers had been in charge of the training of the Turkish army. And German engineers had been driving railroads through the Turkish empire, southeast to Baghdad and south to Medina.

The British, who held Egypt, now found themselves face to face with the Turks in the Sinai Peninsula. Nothing would have suited them better than an Arab revolt. It would have distracted the Turks and given the British an opportunity to launch an attack against Turkish-occupied Palestine.

But the weeks passed into months, the months into years and still the long-awaited rebellion did not come. The desire to throw off the Turkish yoke was strong with both Hussein and his son Feisal. But they feared the terrible Turkish reprisals if they failed—there were 15,000 highly trained Turkish troops in the Hejaz. Hussein and Feisal also feared the destruction of the holy cities of Mecca and Medina. And they were understandably most reluctant to take up arms with Christian Britain against their fellow Moslems, or Mohammedans, as they are often called. The Turks as well as the Arabs were followers of Islam, the religion taught by the Prophet Mohammed in the 600s. Mohammed himself was an Arab, born in Mecca and buried in Medina.

In 1916 word reached Hussein that the Turks were moving many thousands more troops down into the Hejaz. This was the Arabs' last chance. It was then or never, before the odds became too great.

After consultation with the British, Hussein gave the word to his son Feisal, and the Arab Revolt began. Swiftly

Feisal and his Bedouin warriors stormed and took Mecca, the most holy city of the Moslem world. Shortly afterward they captured the Red Sea ports of Jiddah, Rabegh and Yanbo and seized a part of the city of Medina.

It was a brilliant achievement in so short a time, but that was as far as they got. The Turks recaptured the lost section of Medina, destroyed it and slaughtered every man, woman and child there. Down the Hejaz railroad line the Turks poured reinforcements into Medina and greatly strengthened the garrisons guarding the railroad line itself.

Promised British supplies of arms and ammunition never reached Feisal. Soon many of the tribes became disheartened by the lack of British support. Dismayed by the strengthening of the Turkish forces and frankly fearful of the Turkish savagery in reprisals, they began to melt away into the desert.

It began to seem as if the Arab Revolt were over before it had properly begun. Turkey would surely tighten its iron grip even more securely than before, and the dream of Arabian liberation would turn into an endless nightmare of slavery.

And that is what might well have happened had there not then appeared in the Hejaz a twenty-eight-year-old Englishman who was to become legend in his own lifetime—the immortal Lawrence of Arabia.

CHAPTER 2

THE TRAINING OF A DESERT FIGHTER

THOMAS EDWARD LAWRENCE, THE SECOND OF FIVE sons of Anglo-Irish parents, was born in 1888 in Tremadoc, in the country of Caernarvon in North Wales. His father would seem to have been a restless, roving type of man. In the first eight years of T. E. Lawrence's life the family lived in such different places as Scotland, the Isle of Man, the Channel Islands and France as well as Hampshire in southern England. Finally, for the sake of the children's education, the family settled down in Oxford.

Even in the early years of his life, while attending the City of Oxford School, Lawrence displayed qualities

18

which unmistakably marked him out as being apart from his fellows. In his mind and in his behavior, he was completely independent. He was a brilliant scholar, but unlike the average gifted boy he disliked school. He had no interest whatsoever in games of any kind, for organized sports irked and bored his independent mind. His already adventurous spirit vastly preferred exploring the surrounding countryside, taking solitary far-ranging walks—often during the night—and setting off on high-speed long-distance trips on his bicycle.

These activities gave him a strength and a stamina far above the ordinary. And he made use of all his extended excursions to discipline himself to exist for long periods without food, drink or sleep. Why, we do not know. It was almost as if he already knew what his destiny was to be and was already training himself to meet it. In the years to come, in his far-flung travels in the Arabian desert, this endurance and rare ability to go for long periods without food, rest or sleep were to prove invaluable to Lawrence.

Looking back over T. E. Lawrence's early days, one is struck by the strange fact that nearly all his interests, activities and hobbies were exactly the ones he would have chosen had he been consciously aiming toward his ultimate destiny.

Lawrence had the sort of mind that loved to dwell in the romantic past. While still in school he developed two great passions. One was for castles built in the time of the Crusaders; the other was for archaeology—the scientific study of ancient and prehistoric cultures by the excavation of their remains. Both these hobbies he pursued with the relentless concentration that was to become the mark of everything he did in life.

Whenever he had a free day, a free week or a free month, Lawrence went visiting castles or hunting for Roman and medieval potsherds—broken fragments of pottery—on any excavation he found. On all those expeditions he traveled always by bicycle, covering fantastic distances in one day, living on a few pennies and whatever fruit and vegetables came his way.

By the time he was sixteen, Lawrence had visited every twelfth-century castle in England, Wales and France. His interest in those castles led him to a study of military architecture generally. From that he went on to the battles that had been fought around the castles and the campaigns and wars in which those battles had taken place. This in turn led him to the study of other campaigns. Before long the young Lawrence had a knowledge of campaign strategy and tactics that many a general might have envied. It was typical of his thoroughness that, on the practical side, he found time to make himself an expert shot with a revolver!

But his main interest still lay in Crusade castles. In fact, when he went to Oxford University, he decided to offer for his degree thesis a paper on Crusader castles. For this he had to visit and examine for himself the most important Crusader castles of all—those in Syria, where the Crusades against the Mohammedans had actually taken place.

Syria was a wild and rugged land where anything might happen. Against all advice, Lawrence decided to go there alone without what was then considered the very necessary camp equipment and camp followers. He not only went alone but *walked* alone all through Syria—an unheard-of thing for a European. He lived among the poor Arab villagers, sharing their simple and scanty food, getting to know their way of life, their customs, their habits of thought and, increasingly, their language.

During this time he visited and painstakingly examined and photographed no fewer than thirty-seven Syrian Crusader castles. So thoroughly did he study his subject that on his return to England his paper won him a first-class honors degree. Indeed, it was so learned and scholarly that there was said to be difficulty in finding anyone in England competent to judge it.

But Lawrence brought back from Syria more than just information about Crusader castles. He brought back with him the beginnings of the deep sense of mission that was to dominate his entire life in the next dozen years.

He had seen and understood the fear of the Syrian Arabs, witnessed for himself the oppression and brutalities they suffered at the hands of their Turkish overlords. His romantic and sympathetic imagination had already been powerfully seized by the idea of the medieval Crusades. Thus it was only a short step—for Lawrence an almost inevitable step—to become convinced of the need for a modern crusade, a crusade to free the Arabs from their conquerors. But he had not as yet developed any full-fledged plan, nor had he any idea how he would set about achieving his end.

Lawrence was soon to get to know the Arabs even better. He had no sooner finished at Oxford than he was hired by Dr. D. G. Hogarth, the keeper of the Ashmolean Museum at Oxford and a man who had formed a great admiration for Lawrence's work. Hogarth appointed Lawrence to a British Museum expedition on the upper Euphrates in northern Syria. This expedition was engaged in excavating the site of the ancient Hittite city of Carchemish. Here Lawrence was to remain for almost four years, years which he was later to describe as the happiest of his life.

Much is known and recorded of Lawrence's stay in Syria during those years. There can be no doubt but that he proved to be a highly competent archaeologist. There are many tales of his extraordinarily wide circle of friends among the local Arabs, of his ability to get more cooperative work out of them than any other European had ever succeeded in doing. And there are tales of his numerous clashes with the Turkish authorities and the German engineers building the Berlin-Baghdad railroad through the north of Syria.

Unfortunately, there is also much that is not known and not recorded of Lawrence's stay in Syria. These unknown details might throw far greater light on Lawrence's later actions and achievements than all the tales that have been repeated by the many people who have written about him. Far from all of Lawrence's years in the Near East were spent at the Carchemish excavations. The digging there was held up for long periods at a time, mainly owing to seasonal rainfall. During those periods, Lawrence seemed simply to vanish into the desert.

The extent of Lawrence's wanderings in northern Arabia is not known even today. It probably never will be known, for Lawrence wore secrecy like a cloak, telling no one where he had been or where the next day would find him.

It is clear that he must have roamed from the Turkish border down to the Red Sea, from the Mediterranean deep into Mesopotamia. And it is known that he traveled always as an Arab, dressed in Arab clothes, speaking Arabic and living always among the people of the country. And, almost as if he knew that war was inevitable and close, he made highly detailed studies of the strength and disposition of Turkish troops and garrisons throughout northern Arabia.

But one thing can be said with certainty about his journeyings. At the end of them, he knew as much about northern Arabia, the Arabs, their ways of life, their thoughts, their hopes and their dreams as any European alive. Thus even before the outbreak of the First World War, and at the age of only twenty-five, Lawrence was splendidly equipped to meet the destiny that was to be his. He had lived among the poor Arabian people, and out of his first-hand experience had developed a burning sense of mission to lead a campaign, a crusade, to free them from the Turks. He had also made a far-ranging and very detailed study of the art of war. And he knew Arabia and the Arabs better than any professional soldier alive at that time.

But even those qualifications were not enough for a man whose mission it was to lead a crusade for freedom. He also required three other qualifications, each one in its own way as essential as those already named.

He must have courage, not only the physical courage required on a battlefield but the moral courage to make and carry out decisions that might run directly counter to the wishes of his superiors. He must have great will-power. And, perhaps above all, he must have the gift of leadership.

All of those Lawrence had in abundance. His courage and daring in the desert were soon to become a legend. He had tremendous will power and made many enemies among his own fellow officers by his refusal to let anything stand in the way of what he was after. And his quite extraordinary gift for leadership was admitted by practically everyone who ever met him, friend and enemy alike.

This gift of leadership, this ability to inspire on the part of others unquestioning trust and confidence, is impossible to explain. Certainly at a first glance this gift of leadership was difficult to discern in Lawrence. He was a short, rather slight figure with a high forehead, heavy jaw and expression that, in repose, could look not only uninteresting but downright dull. Yet he could, when he so chose, exert an incredible influence over his fellow men. Many distinguished people, including a full-fledged general in the British Army, have gone on record as saying that they would have followed Lawrence to the ends of the earth.

Soon after the outbreak of the First World War

Lawrence, because of his unrivaled knowledge of northern Arabia, found himself posted as an Intelligence Branch officer in Egypt. Unbelievably, in view of his unique gifts, he was to remain desk bound in Cairo for the next twenty-two months. Even after the lapse of so many years it is far from clear why this should have been so.

It may have been that some of his superiors regarded him as indispensable. This could well have been so. When it came to drawing up maps of Turkish-controlled Arabia, providing information on the railroads and roads in those countries or making an accurate judgment of the position and strength of Turkish troops, Lawrence had no superior. And when it came to the questioning of captured Syrians and Palestinians, he certainly had no equal. From a prisoner's face, mannerisms, clothes and accent, Lawrence could usually guess exactly what place he came from. He would casually mention the name of the area and pass a remark about some friends he knew there. Soon the prisoner, convinced that this young English officer knew everything anyway, would tell Lawrence all he wanted to know.

But Lawrence's long stay at his Cairo desk may have been due to another factor—jealousy and downright dislike on the part of his fellow officers and superiors. They may well have been determined that there was to be no promotion for Lawrence, no chance of advancement, of getting out into the desert himself. There have been few famous men in history who have not made enemies as well as friends in the course of their careers, and Lawrence was no exception.

It must be admitted that this was largely his own fault. The slow, plodding, hidebound military minds of the day continually irritated his brilliant intelligence, and he made no attempt to conceal his irritation. Moreover, at that time it was considered essential that a British army officer should be impeccably dressed at all times. Therefore Lawrence's habit of going around without a belt, wearing brown shoes and a colored tie was deeply infuriating to his superiors. But another thing infuriated and provoked them more and caused the greatest resentment. This was the fact that the "young insolent amateur civilian soldier," as they though of him, wrote long and scathing reports of his superiors' conduct of the war in the East. The fact that he was usually perfectly right did not improve matters any.

It may well have been because of this steadily increasing hostility of his superiors that Lawrence was finally transferred from the Intelligence Branch to the Arab Bureau. They may have thought that his activities would be even more limited there, that he would have even less scope for his criticisms and for what they considered his outlandish ideas. But if that is what they thought, then they sadly erred.

The transfer to the Arab Bureau of the Foreign Office was the turning point of Lawrence's life. A government department staffed by both civilians and soldiers, its chief interest lay in a close study of Arabian affairs, especially with a view to fostering among the Arabs a revolt against their Turkish overlords.

It was only a few weeks after Lawrence joined the Bureau that Hussein, the Sherif of Mecca, launched just such a revolt against the Turks. To his third son, Feisal, he entrusted the leading of the main body of the Bedouin tribes. As mentioned earlier, after their initial sweeping successes against the Turks in the summer of 1916, the tide of war began to turn slowly against the Arabs again. It seemed all too likely that the newborn Arab Revolt would be ruthlessly crushed.

At this critical moment Lawrence, on his own initiative—
he was officially on leave at the time—accompanied Sir
Ronald Storrs, a leading official of the Arab Bureau, down
to Jiddah on the Red Sea. They were to consult with the
leaders of the Arab Revolt, and especially with Feisal, the
actual commander of the Arabian forces.

The coming meeting between those two men, the Emir
Feisal and Captain Lawrence, was to be one of the most
momentous and fateful in the long history of the Near East.

CHAPTER 3

FIRST VICTORY

IT WAS NOT FEISAL, BUT ABDULLAH, THE SECOND son of the Sherif of Mecca, whom Lawrence met first on landing at Jiddah. Abdullah was a small stout man, one moment cheerful, the next complaining bitterly about everything. If he had any burning desire to lead his fellow Arabs against the Turkish enemy, he hid it so well that Lawrence dismissed him as no more than a likeable man and a clever politician. Lawrence was already looking for a leader who would unite the Arabian tribes behind him in a crusade against the enemy. And he was convinced that this leader was not to be found in Abdullah.

Two days later, after sailing north to Rabegh, Lawrence met the Sherif's eldest son, Ali. Ali was another great disappointment. He was a fine, kind, gentle man, but very frail and delicate in health, already growing old at the age of thirty-seven. Lawrence quickly realized that this was not the man to stand up to the cruel rigors of extended campaigns in the desert.

But another two days later, after a long camel ride into the interior to the town of Hamra, Lawrence found his man at last—the Emir Feisal ibn Hussein, third son of the Sherif of Mecca.

Lawrence has left an account of his first meeting with Feisal and the immediate impression Feisal made upon him. "I felt at first glance," Lawrence says, "that this was the man I had come to Arabia to seek—the leader who would bring the Arab Revolt to full glory. Feisal looked very tall and pillar-like, very slender, in his long white silk robes and his brown head-cloth bound with a brilliant scarlet and gold cord. His eyelids were dropped; and his black beard and colorless face were like a mask against the strange, still watchfulness of his body."

No question but that Feisal made an immediate and great impact on Lawrence. It would have been surprising had he not. Thirty-one years old, graceful and regal in appearance, quick and vigorous in all his actions, clever, hot-tempered, impatient, very proud, he was idolized by the fierce Bedouin tribesmen whom he led. For Lawrence he was the ideal and heaven-sent choice for a commander-in-chief who would lead his people to freedom.

There is no account of Feisal's reaction to Lawrence, but it must have been a very strong and favorable one. For, though Lawrence was only a very junior army officer and Feisal was a king's son and commander in chief, they spent much time that same day and night discussing the military situation. They also discussed what form British aid to the Arabian forces should take. This was the most urgent problem of the moment.

A look at Feisal's troops next morning helped Lawrence make up his mind on this point. He recorded: "They are a tough-looking crowd, all very dark-coloured. . . . they go about bristling with cartridge belts and fire off their rifles when they can. As for their physical condition, I doubt whether I have ever seen men harder."

Here, Lawrence immediately realized, were ideal guerrilla troops. These were men who could hit and run, who could strike hard and swiftly, then vanish on camel-back into the fastnesses of the desert where no Turk could ever hope to find them. It would be folly, and a criminal waste, Lawrence felt, to use such men in the static, conventional warfare of that day.

In 1916 military tactics were very different even from those used in the Second World War. The ideal of warfare in World War I was to have great masses of men lined up against one another in roughly parallel trenches with only a narrow strip of no man's land between them. The battles consisted of those great tightly packed hordes of men—as many as a million in a single battle—pounding one another in close-range terrible massacre until one side or the other broke.

Lawrence knew that the Arabs were the last people on earth to engage in such a type of warfare. He also knew that in spite of their splendid courage in individual, hand-to-hand open combat, they lacked discipline. And he shrewdly suspected that they would be unable to stand up to the continuous heavy-shelling—and, increasingly, bombing—that was so much a part of the grim lives of the men in the trenches on the Western Front in Europe.

Moreover Lawrence was all too clearly aware that his superiors in Cairo still had, for the most part, the old-fashioned military cast of mind. They believed trench warfare to be the most modern and up-to-date type of all. The British troops in Egypt were, in the main, trained for just this type of fighting. The possibility of British and Arabs fighting successfully side by side just did not exist. The Arabs, as fighters, had as much in common with the British soldiers as the American Indians had with Braddock's redcoats whom they massacred so mercilessly at the battle of Fort Duquesne.

Then there was the religious question to be kept in mind. Many of the proud, independent Bedouin tribes had by no means yet decided to help King Hussein and his son Feisal in the fight for Arabian independence. And Lawrence felt that, if British troops were landed in Arabia to fight the Turks, those uncommitted tribes might object strongly. They would not like the idea of bringing in Christians to help fight the Turks who, for all their faults, were Moslems like themselves. And neither Hussein nor Feisal was at all keen on having large numbers of Christian troops in the Hejaz. For this is the Holy Land for all Moslems throughout the world.

Enemies and critics of Lawrence have since suggested that his real reason for not wanting British troops in Arabia was that such troops would be commanded by officers very senior to himself. Then he, Lawrence, would have to fade very much into the background and take no further part in the direction of the Arabian revolt.

This is an unfair accusation, with no evidence to lend it strength. Apart from religious difficulties and the unsuitability of having British soldiers fight along with the Arabs, Lawrence did not want British troops in Arabia for a simple reason. His heart was in Arabian independence and he feared that this would never be achieved if the British took over direction of the revolt. He saw no prospects of future independence for the Arabs if the rule of the Turks was only going to be replaced by that of the British. Independence could be achieved only if the Arabs fought and won the war by themselves.

Accordingly, Lawrence wrote a long report to his superiors in Cairo, setting forth the situation as he saw it and strongly recommending against sending any British troops to the Hejaz. All that was required, he said, was a handful of British officers to assist in training the Arabs in some of the more advanced techniques of modern warfare, especially in the use of explosives and demolitions.

To what must have been Lawrence's vast astonishment, his report was enthusiastically welcomed among the senior officers who had so recently sought an excuse to get rid of him. It was welcomed, of course only because his conclusions seemed to coincide so exactly with their own wishes.

As far as British headquarters in Cairo was concerned, the only war that mattered was the one being fought with the Turks in Palestine. The British did not want to fritter away their resources by sending troops to open another front in the Hejaz. So grateful were they, indeed, that they actually made Lawrence official liaison officer with Feisal's army.

There were probably two reasons for this. The first was that Cairo headquarters was perfectly aware of the advantage it would be to have the Arabian tribes operating in the rear of the Turkish armies. Though the British were reluctant to spare any of their own troops for use in Arabia, it would be more than useful to have one of their own men in Feisal's camp to keep them in touch with developments. And despite the many faults Lawrence had in their eyes, no officer in the Near East was better suited to deal with the Arabs than he was. The other reason for making him a liaison officer was probably that it suited Cairo very well indeed to have such a thorn in the flesh as far away as possible!

Nothing could have pleased Lawrence more, although it cannot be said that he took his position as liaison officer very seriously. A liaison officer can be defined as a person who is a link or means of communication between two parties. But Lawrence didn't see himself in this role at all. Already he was seeing himself as the power behind the scenes, the all-but-invisible figure in the background who held the reins that guided Feisal and, along with him, the whole Arabian liberation movement.

Lawrence wasted no time. Soon after his return from Cairo, in January of 1917, Lawrence, Feisal and Colonel S.F. Newcombe were on their way north to attack the Turkish-held port of Wejh. Meanwhile 500 Arabs aboard British naval vessels were en route to attack Wejh under cover of bombardment from the sea.

The ensuing fight for the port of Wejh has often been described as Lawrence's first victory in the desert campaigns. In point of fact it was nothing of the kind. Lawrence had not yet achieved any position of importance in Feisal's army, and the town was taken after a very brief skirmish by Arabs landing from the British warships. It happened two days before Feisal and Lawrence even appeared on the scene.

In passing, it might be recorded that the Turkish governor of the town, seeing the British warships closing in, made an impassioned speech and appeal to his garrison troops. He urged each and every soldier to fight to the death for the sake of their Turkish homeland. After finishing this stirring address to his troops, the gallant governor waited until darkness fell. Then he fled for his life, leaving his men to face the enemy alone.

But if it wasn't an important battle, it at least had important results. First of all, it made the British High Command take the Arab Revolt into serious consideration. Also, all the major Red Sea ports in the Hejaz were now in the hands of the Arabs. News of this victory, little though it had cost, spread abroad. Tribesmen throughout the Hejaz and beyond flocked to join Feisal's banner. With Wejh secured, the Arabs were free to extend the war of liberation against the Turks.

The Arab leaders were convinced that the next stage of

the war should be directed against the destruction of the Turks still occupying the city of Medina. Medina, after Mecca, was the most holy city in the Mohammedan world. And how could the Arabs hope to regard the war in the Hejaz as won, how could they think of attacking the Turks on other fronts while a great city in the heart of their homeland was still in the hands of the enemy? British headquarters in Cairo was of the same opinion. So Lawrence was sent to Abdullah, Feisal's elder brother who was at that time in the neighborhood of Medina, to urge an immediate attack on that city.

Fortunately for the course of the Arabian war, Lawrence fell violently ill from dysentery on the 150-mile ride to Abdullah's camp. Indeed he was so ill that he barely managed to reach his destination. And after joining Abdullah, he lay for more than a week helpless and unable to move in his tent. This period of inactivity gave him invaluable time to think out the future course of the desert war.

It did not take Lawrence long to arrive at the conclusion that an attack on Medina would be military folly of the first order. Medina was at the very southern end of the German-built, Turkish-controlled Hejaz railroad that stretched all the way north to Damascus and beyond. All the food, supplies, guns, ammunition and reinforcements necessary to maintain the very large Medina garrison came by this route and this route alone.

If the Turks were driven out of Medina, what then? There would be only one thing they could do—retreat north along the Hejaz railroad, gathering up en route the many thousands of men who were required to guard the line. They would not be able to feel even reasonably safe until they were north of the Dead Sea. By that time the numbers of retreating Turks, all first-class fighting troops, would have swollen to twenty or thirty thousand men—a whole new army to be used against the Egypt-based British forces.

How much better it would be, Lawrence reasoned, to leave the Turks in Medina, without attacking them at all. Then with a few small hand-picked bands of raiding Arabs under British demolition experts it should be possible to cut the Hejaz railroad at cautiously calculated intervals. If it were cut too often, the number of supplies reaching the Medina garrison would dwindle to a mere trickle. Then the Turks in starved desperation would be compelled to fight their way out, northward, thus defeating the object of the plan. But the railroad would have to be cut at frequent enough intervals to force the Turks to maintain large repair gangs along the 700-mile stretch. Also the Turks would need very many more troops, at least 10,000, to man the numerous garrison points strung out along the length of the Hejaz railroad.

It was a brilliant idea, completely at odds with the accepted military thinking of the time—which said, in effect, that any mass of the enemy should be destroyed wherever found. And the idea was to have all the splendid success it so richly deserved. All through the war, Turkish garrisons and repair gangs struggled desperately to keep the Hejaz railroad open. And in that way a mere handful of Bedouins succeeded in tying down over 30,000 Turkish troops, who were as good as lost to their commander in chief when it came to fighting the main campaign against the British.

Lawrence left Abdullah without ever revealing the true reason for his visit and returned to Feisal's camp. In his usual indirect but highly persuasive fashion he managed to get the Arab leaders to accept his new viewpoint, and he immediately set about organizing regular attacks on the Hejaz railroad. The object of these attacks was to blow up

sections of the track—particularly curved stretches where
the rails to repair the damage had to be brought down all
the way from Damascus. Of course the supreme ambition
was to blow up the tracks just as a troop or supply train for
the Medina garrison was passing over them. But always
Lawrence and his men had to be careful. Trains carrying
Moslem pilgrims to Mecca ran even in wartime. To have
blown up a trainload of the faithful on pilgrimage would
have done the British and Arabian cause untold harm.

But though successful, the attacks on the railroad were
a purely negative affair. Lawrence and his men could keep
on blowing up the Hejaz railroad for a hundred years
without ending the war. Lawrence felt that Feisal's forces
must make a more direct contribution to victory. And that
could be done only by moving north against the main body
of the Turkish armies holding Syria and Palestine. But for
this they would require a base, a seaport. From such a base
Feisal's army could be supplied by ships from the Royal
Navy with food, arms and ammunition—not to mention
large quantities of gold for bribing wavering Bedouin
tribes to join the revolt.

Lawrence turned his eyes toward Aqaba.

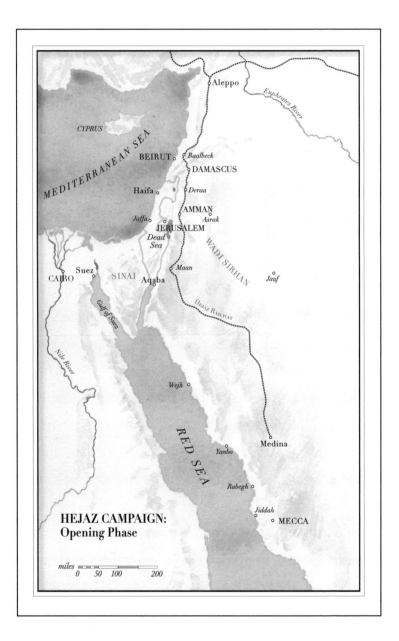

HEJAZ CAMPAIGN:
Opening Phase

miles
0   50   100   200

CHAPTER 4

THE MARCH ON AQABA

LAWRENCE REALIZED THAT AQABA, A DEEP-WATER
port lying at the tip of the northeastern arm of the Red Sea,
would be an ideal base for further operations against the
Turks. But there was one immediate drawback. It would
have to be captured first. For Aqaba was in the hands of a
Turkish garrison.

Capturing it, Lawrence was aware, would not be easy.
For he was well acquainted with Aqaba and knew that it
would be impossible to take the port from the direction
of the sea or from along either coast.

Lawrence knew Aqaba because, just before the war, the British had entrusted Colonel Newcombe with the carrying out of a military survey in the Sinai peninsula, which included Aqaba. As a cover and to disarm suspicion, they had summoned Lawrence from Carchemish to accompany Newcombe. This was to deceive the Turks into thinking that the expedition was an archaeological exploration instead of the spying venture that it really was.

The deception hadn't been as successful as the British had hoped, and the two men had been roughly handled by the Turks. But Lawrence had found out enough to know that, because of the gorges and defiles with which Aqaba was all but surrounded, it could be taken only from the rear.

There were three further difficulties.

The first was that Feisal's troops were reluctant to venture so far from home among possibly hostile tribes. Lawrence, however, knew he could rely on Feisal to bring his army north once the port was taken.

The second difficulty was that, since tribes would have to be recruited for the attack in the north, there would have to be a base for operations. The only feasible base in that barren and waterless desert was the Wadi Sirhan, a 200-mile string of oases between Azrak on the Syrian border and Jauf. But before they could use the water holes as a base, permission would have to be obtained from the powerful Emir of Ruwalla.

The third difficulty was that the permission could be obtained and the tribes recruited by one man and one man only. This was the far-famed Auda, the great warrior chief of the clan of the Howietat Bedouin.

The first requirement, obviously, was to have Auda on the spot. He was asked to come and confer with Feisal and Lawrence, and come he did, without any loss of time. Once he heard that there was the prospect of a fight, it would doubtless have been impossible to stop him.

Sheik Auda abu Tayi was a living legend. No longer a young man—he was about fifty—Auda was huge, gaunt and swarthy. He had a great beaming smile that vanished only when he solemnly told the most monstrous and atrocious lies about events and people's characters. He was beyond all doubt the greatest desert fighter of his time—and very possibly of all time. From Kurdistan to the Arabian Sea his fame was exceeded only by the universal fear in which he was held. Even kings walked softly when Auda abu Tayi passed by.

To Auda war was life and life was war; it was as simple as that. Every chieftain in northern Arabia went in constant terror of him in case he took it into his head to raid them. And he had attacked practically every tribe between Aleppo on the Turkish border and Basra on the Persian Gulf, just as the whim took him. He had married twenty-eight times, been wounded thirteen times, seen all his tribesmen injured in battle and nearly all his relations killed. Within the previous fifteen years, he had with his own hand killed seventy-five men. A mere fraction of the total count, this did not include the large numbers of Turks he had dispatched, for Auda reckoned them not worth the counting.

It said much, incidentally, for Auda's respect for Feisal and his desire for Arabian independence that he had temporarily given up at least a dozen feuds he was carrying on with neighboring chieftains. He had done this in order to consider ways and means of attacking the Turk, a man he considered beneath contempt as a fighting foe.

Typical of Auda's impulsiveness and flamboyance was

his action on the night of his arrival at the meeting with Feisal and Lawrence. In the middle of a meal he suddenly rose, dashed out of the tent, removed his false teeth and smashed them to pieces as a symbol of his undying enmity to the Turkish overlords. The reason: the false teeth had been made in Turkey.

As a man to have on the Arab-British side in what promised to be a hard and bitterly fought desert campaign, there was no one in the world who could compare with Auda. Lawrence and he took to each other at once and were to remain more or less side by side and inseparable friends until the end of the war.

Soon Lawrence and Auda, accompanied by Sherif Nasir—a relative of Feisal's, who was in nominal command of the expedition—set out for the Wadi Sirhan. This region lay 200 miles to the east of their final objective, Aqaba. The long journey across the Arabian desert—about 350 miles in all—is typical of the scores of such journeys that Lawrence made during the war.

They set out on camels heavily laden with stores. These included high explosives for blowing up sections of the

Hejaz railroad, which they would have to cross on their way to the Sirhan. Then there were great 45-pound bags of flour, each of which would keep one man going for five or six weeks. And Lawrence was taking more than £20,000 in gold to persuade wavering tribes to join them.

At first their route lay through a burning desert of pure white sand. The reflection of the sun on the gleaming sand hurt their eyes as cruelly as the dazzle from frozen snow. Water there was none; they had to carry their own. But the toughened Bedouin could go for an entire day without water and get by with only a pint on the second. Lawrence, dressed as always like an Arab in his hooded, flowing white robes, rode uncomplainingly on camel-back with the best of the Bedouins (Only those who have tried it can appreciate how horribly uncomfortable camel riding can be.) He sought for no favors for himself in the way of food and water. The toughening of his early youth, where he had trained himself in stoical endurance and the ability to go without food and drink, was paying off indeed.

Then they entered a region of red sandstone, furnace-hot in the pitiless white glare of that sun. It was so hot that several camels eventually weakened and died and had to be cut up for meat. This sandstone was followed by long, indescribably bleak and barren stretches of lava, where both men and animals suffered tortures of heat and thirst. Finally they came to an oasis, with water and shade, but even here their troubles were not over. As happened so often to Lawrence in Arabia, they were attacked by hostile tribesmen. These hostile Bedouins had, of course, no means of knowing that the very men they were attacking were those who would at last bring freedom to their land.

The long, bitter, exhausting ride went on. They came to the Hejaz railroad, where they blew up sections of the line and destroyed the telephone wires. Lawrence tells us how on this occasion the tireless and indestructible Auda composed a long poem in praise of the dynamite that had wrought such damage to the railroad!

Then on again they went into the depths of the desert, a desert that was at times of hardened shining mud that hurt their eyes even more cruelly than the reflected light from white sand. Sometimes vast stretches of sand itself were whipped up by the burning wind into a driving, scorching, stinging wall of a million flying needles. It blinded men and camels alike and brought visibility down to only a few feet. But those men were Bedouin, men who could survive in incredibly cruel, desperate conditions that would have killed almost any European—all but Lawrence. He was as enduring, as immune to pain and thirst and exhaustion as the iron men who traveled by his side. They rode steadily on.

After two weeks of this brutally inhuman riding, Lawrence had an opportunity to prove to the Bedouins that he was as tough and tireless as any Arab alive. They were trudging along through the sand—they had dismounted to save the strength of their exhausted camels—blinded by the driving sand and weak from heat and lack of water. Sometime during the day Lawrence saw that one of the party was missing. To turn back, weak and worn out as he now was, into that sand-swept unmarked wilderness, could have been just another way of committing suicide. But Lawrence turned back to look for the missing man. And he turned back alone.

By one chance in a thousand Lawrence found the man, exhausted, blinded and half dead from thirst, took him in charge and turned back again to rejoin the party. Even then Lawrence might have been lost, might have failed to find his friends in that blind and featureless wilderness of flying sand. The saga of Lawrence of Arabia would then have ended before it had properly begun. But Auda, who had noticed Lawrence's absence, turned back and found him. After this, Lawrence's prestige among the Bedouins was secure for all time.

A few days later—eighteen days after the beginning of this journey—they reached the Howietat area where Auda's tribesmen lived. Even in those last few days they had run into constant trouble, losing men from snipers' bullets and snake bites. The Howietat area was alive with poisonous snakes and the local cure for such a bite was to cover the wound with snakeskin and read chapters of the Koran over the invalid. After a few hours of this, the unfortunate sufferer almost invariably died.

Sheik Auda now went ahead to rouse his tribesmen and get the permission of the Emir of Ruwalla to use the Wadi Sirhan as a base. He took along with him £6,000 in gold to help the Emir to make up his mind.

While Auda was doing this, Lawrence undertook a strange long ride to the north, far beyond Damascus. He rode alone.

Lawrence's solitary excursion into the heart of Turkish-occupied territory remains a mystery. If any man knows or ever has known the reason for this journey, or the details of it, he has kept silent. So did Lawrence. In his famous book of the Arabian war, *Seven Pillars of Wisdom*, there is no mention whatsoever made of it.

The only certain fact that seems to be known is that he blew up a bridge at Baalbek, on the Damascus-Aleppo railroad—the northern continuation of the Hejaz railroad. Beyond that fact, all is guesswork. It is said that he conferred with revolutionary-minded leaders in Syria to see how ready they were to join the Arab cause. And it is said that he dropped many hints, without being too careful about his choice of confidants, that the Arabs would be operating up north in the Damascus direction before very long.

It is highly probable that Lawrence was seeking to give the impression—to which the blowing up of the bridge added—that the next thrust of the Arabs would be toward Damascus, the heart of Turkish Arabia. This impression would effectively prevent the Turks from even beginning to have any suspicions about a forthcoming attack on Aqaba.

This guess is confirmed by what happened on his return when he was met by the Emir of Ruwalla. In spite—or perhaps because—of the £6,000 he had received from Auda, the Emir was still very nervous. He feared what might happen to him if the Turks found out that Arabian tribes were mustering in his Wadi Sirhan. Lawrence told him that he was to worry about it no longer. On the contrary, he should at once inform the Turks of the presence of the gathering Arab forces!

The Emir's astonishment can be imagined; but Lawrence's point is easily seen. A glance at the map on page 75 will show that the northern part of the Sirhan is as near to Damascus as it is to Aqaba. The known presence of Arab forces there would almost certainly be thought by the Turks to herald an attack on Damascus. Their first reaction to the news would be to prepare to intercept the Arabs on their supposed northward march from the Sirhan. And by sending troops to block this nonexistent attack the Turks would leave the way wide open to the southwest for the attack on Aqaba.

There was no question about it: Lawrence was a master of intrigue and deception.

To increase the deception still further, Lawrence and a picked band of men set out from the Wadi Sirhan and reached the railroad line in the vicinity of Deraa, halfway between the Sirhan and Damascus. They blew up the track there, derailed a train and captured a Turkish-manned station. There could be no doubt now in the minds of the enemy that the Bedouins were heading for Damascus.

But quickly the Arabs wheeled and thrust south for their original target—Aqaba. On the way there they heard that a squadron of 400 Turkish cavalry was hunting for them. The news didn't worry Lawrence overmuch, for the same messenger told them that a local sheik had thoughtfully provided the Turks with a guide who was leading them in a completely wrong direction.

Then came a serious holdup in their plans. They learned that they were not going to be able to thrust straight on to Aqaba. The blockhouse at Abu el Lissal, which lay on a direct line between Maan and Aqaba, was in the hands of the enemy.

As planned beforehand, this enemy blockhouse had been taken by another detachment of Arabs. But by sheer bad luck an entire battalion of Turkish troops happened to be within a few miles at the time. They heard of the capture of the blockhouse, advanced on it, retook it in a massed attack and drove off the occupying Arab tribesmen. Then, by way of revenge, they went out to a little, unsuspecting Arab encampment in the neighborhood and killed everyone there, women and children included.

Such was the situation that Lawrence, Auda and Sherif Nasir found at their arrival. Their feelings at discovering the massacre can be imagined. They immediately besieged the blockhouse, pouring in a heavy fire on the defenders. But so well placed were the Turks, so determinedly did they fight back that it seemed impossible they could ever be dislodged. But dislodged they were, and by so small a thing as an insult offered Auda by Lawrence.

In the middle of the day, when it was so intolerably hot that most of the Arabs could fire only very occasionally, Auda came to Lawrence. He pointed to his own still rapidly firing clansmen and asked proudly: "What think ye of the Howietat now?"

"Indeed," Lawrence replied, "they shoot a lot and hit a little."

Auda stared at him, then ripped off his headcloth in berserk rage and dashed it to the ground. Shouting at Lawrence, "Get your camel if you want to see the old man's work," he rushed away shouting hoarsely for his tribesmen to follow him. Before Lawrence could stop him Auda was leading fifty horsemen in a breakneck suicidal downhill charge against the enemy.

There was nothing for the horrified Lawrence and Nasir to do but mount their camels, gather 400 tribesmen and charge after him. Lawrence, on a famous racing camel, soon outdistanced the rest. He was rapidly overtaking Auda and his men, who had already smashed headlong into the Turkish positions, when his camel was shot through the head. Lawrence was pitched a great distance forward over the dying animal's head, to crash unconscious to the ground. He should at least have broken some limbs or ribs—if not his neck—but Lawrence, as the Arabs were beginning to discover, was very tough indeed.

When he recovered consciousness, the battle was over. The Arabs, mad for revenge, had killed 300 Turks and taken 150 more as prisoners—in return for the loss of exactly two of their own men. It was incredible.

The spectacle of the triumphant Sheik Auda, when he came to ask Lawrence what he thought of his Howietat tribesmen now, was even more incredible. One bullet had smashed his treasured field glasses, another had pierced his pistol holster, others had reduced his sword scabbard to mangled strips of leather. Six more had passed through his clothing, and his horse had been shot dead under him. But Auda himself was completely unharmed. Even for a man supposed to bear the charmed life Auda did, it was indeed a miracle. Auda himself gave the entire credit for his survival to a copy of the Koran, which he always carried with him.

It is an interesting sidelight on the basic simplicity of this amazing man that his Koran was a cheap reproduction made in Glasgow and sold for exactly eighteen pence— about twenty cents. Many years previously some unscrupulous salesman had talked Auda into paying £120 for it—at that time, about $600!

From Abu el Lissal the Arab forces pressed on to Aqaba. And the capture of Aqaba, after the fight at the block-house, turned out to be a complete anticlimax. Many more tribesmen, swayed by this latest Arab victory, had flocked to join Lawrence's banner on the last stages of the march. The Turkish garrison at Aqaba, who were already being bombarded from the sea, had heard of the fate of their comrades at Abu el Lissal. So when they saw the hordes of Arabs advancing upon them, they surrendered without even the semblance of a fight.

Aqaba was now in the hands of the Arabs. The Army of Revolt had secured a base and the way was open for a thrust into the heartland of the enemy.

CHAPTER 5

GUERILLA WARFARE

EXHAUSTED THOUGH HE WAS—HE HAD BEEN averaging fifty miles a day on camel-back for many weeks now—Lawrence did not remain very long in Aqaba. He couldn't, unless he wanted a famine on his hands. For besides 500 of his own men, there were now in Aqaba 2,000 newfound Bedouin allies and 700 prisoners. All of these men had to be fed, and Lawrence had no means whatsoever of feeding them.

He remained in Aqaba only long enough to secure the city against recapture by setting up strong defensive positions in the rocky defiles leading into the port from the rear. Then Lawrence set off with a small band of picked companions, the toughest he could find, mounted on the finest camels available, across the barren blazing waste of the Sinai desert toward Suez. Making their way through 150 miles of unimaginable hardship with only one watering hole on the way, they reached Suez in exactly fifty hours. From Suez Lawrence took a train to Ismailia. When the news of his great success was made known to the military authorities there, a warship, the *Dufferin*, packed full with supplies and provisions, was immediately sent to Aqaba.

It was during this very brief stay in Egypt that Lawrence met with the British general, Edmund H. H. Allenby, with whom his name was to be so closely linked for the remainder of the war. Allenby, nicknamed "The Bull," had arrived from the Western Front only a few days before to become commander in chief of the British army in Egypt.

Rarely could the arrival of fresh blood in the shape of a new commander have been more welcomed. Things were going badly indeed for the British in the Near East. They were completely bogged down in their war against the Turks. Allenby's arrival brought an entirely new and much needed spirit of confidence to the jaded British army.

It is rather uncertain what impression Allenby and Lawrence, two utterly different men, made on each other. The one was big, burly, clad in the immaculate and much-decorated uniform of an army general. The other was small, deeply sunburned, wasted away from hardship and hunger, dressed in flowing Arab robes and bare of foot. Accounts of their meeting vary. But evidently both men immediately understood each other as soldiers. They found that their points of view on campaign strategy and tactics to be employed in campaigns were very similar indeed. Allenby, though fresh from the Western Front, was no Western Front general. Indeed, he had strongly expressed his distaste for the static mass killing of trench warfare and the immovably fixed and hidebound mentalities of the generals who directed this warfare. And it may well have been because of this that he was sent out to Egypt, where he could no longer annoy his commander in chief.

Allenby was first and foremost an old-fashioned

cavalry man whose heart lay not in trench warfare but in mobility, surprise, complete freedom of movement and the use of irregular guerrilla warfare. It is little wonder, therefore, that he and Lawrence found themselves in perfect agreement on the way the war against the Turks should be waged. Broadly, they agreed that while the main British armies fought their way up the Palestine coast, Lawrence and his Arabs should remain to the east of the Dead Sea and the River Jordan. There they were to ease Allenby's task as much as possible by continually harassing the enemy from the rear.

Allenby gave complete and immediate proof of the confidence he had in the young Lawrence. The latter, still only a 28-year-old junior officer, asked Allenby for £200,000—a million dollars—in gold. This was to win over the loyalty of still wavering Arab chieftains and pay his own troops. Allenby gave it to him at once and without question. Indeed, he was better than his word; he eventually gave Lawrence more than £500,000—and the disposal of this money was to be entirely Lawrence's responsibility. It was a splendid gesture of trust and faith in so young a man.

It was also agreed between the two men that the main Arab army under Feisal should be brought north from the Hejaz to Aqaba. It was to come under the overall control of Allenby, while being allowed to act independently under Feisal and Lawrence.

To achieve this it was necessary to have the agreement and permission of two men—Feisal and his father Hussein, the Sherif of Mecca. Lawrence was almost certain that Feisal would agree, for he knew how impatient Feisal was at having to remain in the Hejaz, far from the scene of the main fighting. Whether Hussein would be willing to allow the army, which was, after all, *his* army, to move out of the Hejaz and so out of his control, was another question altogether.

Lawrence determined to see both men as soon as possible. The *Dufferin*, newly returned from Aqaba, was assigned to carry Lawrence, now a be-medaled and newly promoted major, down the Red Sea. He disembarked at Wejh and flew to Jeida, an inland town where Feisal now had his base. As expected, he had no difficulty in getting Feisal's enthusiastic consent to the move of the Arab army north to Aqaba.

While he was in Jeida, Lawrence learned of the continuing success of the raiding parties against the Hejaz railroad. Scarcely a day passed without some section of the railroad being torn or blown up. Scarcely a week went by without a train being derailed or destroyed. Newcombe, Joyce and Davenport were keeping the Turkish repair squads and garrison troops busily occupied.

Newcombe, especially, was tireless. The Arabs complained bitterly of how exhausting it was to work under him. "Newcombe," they said "is like fire. He burns friend and enemy." As Lawrence himself remarked, Newcombe did four times as much as any other Englishman would have done and ten times as much as the exhausted Arabs under him thought necessary.

As well satisfied with his visit to Jeida as he had been with his visit to Egypt, Lawrence flew back to Wejh, boarded the *Dufferin* again and sailed south to Jiddah. There he met Hussein, who had made a special trip from Mecca to meet him. To Lawrence's surprise and relief the meeting passed off well: Hussein gave his consent to the northward move of the Arab army.

But if Lawrence was pleased with this, he was far from

pleased by the contents of a cable just received from Cairo. The cable said that Intelligence agents had discovered that Auda was negotiating with the Turks with a view to abandoning the Arabs and going over to the Turkish side. Nor was there any doubt about the truth of the report. The agents had actually captured some of the correspondence that had passed between Auda and the enemy.

This was grave news indeed. Auda was the keystone in the defense of Aqaba; if he withdrew, all was lost. Lawrence immediately set sail for Aqaba and confronted Auda with his knowledge.

Auda, as has already been mentioned, had a genius for telling the most magnificent and convincing lies. He solemnly assured Lawrence that it was all part of an elaborate joke he was playing on the unsuspecting Turks. Lawrence pretended to enter into the joke. But when he casually repeated, as if they were his own words, long stretches of the correspondence that had passed between Auda and the Turks, Auda grew thoughtful. When Lawrence mentioned that Feisal and the Arab army were en route to Aqaba, Auda grew still more thoughtful. When Lawrence said that Allenby was sending them large quantities of ammunition, guns and supplies, Auda stopped joking about his correspondence with the Turks.

Lawrence finally mentioned that Allenby was sending large amounts of money to Aqaba and an immediate advance of £1,000 in gold. When Auda heard that, he put very firmly out of his mind any intentions he might ever have had of going over to the enemy. An astute business-man, Auda knew on which side his bread was buttered.

And so Auda was persuaded to remain as the keystone in Aqaba's defense during the weeks it took to bring the Arab army under Feisal north to that port. The transfer was completed by August 23rd.

Nor was it completed a day too soon. The Turks were keenly aware of the serious threat to their rear with the Arab army based in so forward a position as Aqaba. So they were pouring troops down the railroad from Damascus, building up their forces for an all-out assault on the port.

The Turks now had 6,000 troops at Maan, the nearest main station on the line, as well as 2,000 at Abu el Lissal, between Maan and Aqaba. And they had brought down an entire cavalry regiment from Palestine. That left only two such regiments to meet the main assault planned by Allenby in Palestine.

This was exactly what Lawrence and Allenby had had in mind when they worked out their tactics together. The threat from the rear was causing the Turks to pull thousands of first-class fighting troops out of Palestine—at least 10,000 in this case. More than that number were already marooned hundreds of miles away in Medina or assigned to guard the Hejaz railroad. It would be a fair estimate to say that Lawrence's maneuvers drew as many as 25,000 first-line Turkish troops away from the main Palestine front at the crucial moment when Allenby attacked. This was approximately one quarter of their total strength south of the city of Damascus.

As far as Allenby was concerned, Lawrence had already more than fulfilled his purpose. Lawrence, too, knew this but was in no mind to congratulate himself yet. He had a much more immediate concern: to keep himself from being crushed by the offensive he knew the Turks were preparing against Aqaba. And the Turks had a great superiority both in manpower and firepower.

The methods Lawrence adopted to prevent this all-out

assault against Aqaba were completely typical of the man. Always, for Lawrence, the best, the *only* method of defense was attack—but never a direct attack against the main body of the enemy troops.

There was no need for a frontal assault on the main Turkish positions at Maan and Abu el Lissal to prevent mounting an attack on Aqaba. Exactly the same end could be achieved, and at infinitely less cost in life, by maintaining a nonstop around-the-clock guerrilla warfare against them. First there would be a swift attack from the direction from which it was expected—a feint here, a jab there. Then there would be an unexpected bombing attack on a barracks, the demolition of a railway bridge or the capture of a station on the Hejaz railroad. A hundred such prods against the enemy—swift, silent, over almost as soon as they had begun—kept the Turks anxious and worried. Continuously on edge, they never knew where the next blow might fall.

They never knew where and when the camel-borne Arabs would come storming out of the desert at dawn. They never knew whether the next attack might be made with a dozen Arabs—or with a thousand. Were Feisal and

Lawrence concentrating their troops for an advance on Maan, on Abu el Lissal or even Amman? The Turks had no means of knowing, no means of even beginning to guess.

They were completely unable to cope with those will-o'-the-wisp desert fighters who sprang so magically from the empty desert and as mysteriously disappeared again. The Turks felt that their only hope of safety lay in keeping their troops together in large masses in fortified positions. Only then could they deal with the Bedouin. This meant, of course, that the Turkish forces, with their great superiority in numbers, remained completely inactive. Their will to move was quite paralyzed by the repeated pinprick attacks from every quarter of the compass.

But, just in case they might lash out in final desperation, Lawrence proceeded to immobilize the enemy almost completely. He personally led many daring raids on the railroad line north and south of the main Turkish position at Maan. In a few weeks, a score of engines, uncounted railroad trucks and miles of track were destroyed. Great quantities of booty, food and ammunition were captured and many Turkish soldiers killed.

It became almost impossible for fresh supplies and reinforcements to reach the Turkish forces. And without those it was equally impossible for the Turks to mount an attack.

This new and wholesale destruction of the railroad line had still another purpose. When Allenby's attack was launched in Palestine, the Turks would find it impossible to bring up reinforcements from the Medina garrison and Hejaz railroad, even if they wanted to. And Allenby's attack was about to begin.

The time had come, Lawrence felt, when he could give Allenby even more direct support than provided by the immobilization of one quarter of the entire Turkish army, invaluable though that help was. Lawrence no longer feared an attack on Aqaba. The Turks were in such a state of anxiety and confusion that the possibility had almost vanished. When Allenby launched his assault, within the next week or two, the enemy would have far more to think of than the capture of Aqaba.

Once again, Lawrence turned his eyes to the north.

CHAPTER 6

FAILURE AND SUCCESS

SOME 250 MILES NORTH OF AQABA AND 80 MILES
south of Damascus lay the town of Deraa, an important
junction on the Hejaz railroad. It was, in fact, the most
important junction on the whole of the 1,000-mile stretch
from Aleppo in the north to Medina in the south.

West from Deraa ran a narrow-gauge railroad to the south
of the Sea of Galilee and on to Haifa on the Mediterranean
coast. From there a broad-gauge railroad ran south to Jaffa,
Gaza and Jerusalem. It was down this broad-gauge railroad
that all supplies came for the Turkish army stretched out on

a broad front between Gaza on the coast and the Dead Sea.

But before reaching this broad-gauge railroad every ton of supplies, all arms and ammunition, every soldier had first to travel along the narrow-gauge railroad between Deraa and Haifa. It was the only means of communication between Damascus and the Turkish front.

This was the railroad Lawrence was now determined to cut. If this line were blown up, it would be impossible for the Turks to bring any more reinforcements to their army when the British attack on Palestine began. And it would also make large-scale escape impossible.

The place Lawrence chose was the wild and rocky gorge of the Yarmuk, between Deraa and the Sea of Galilee. The stream tumbling down this deep and winding valley was crossed and recrossed many times by high bridges. Blow up one of those bridges and the line would be out of action for weeks.

When informed of Lawrence's plan, Allenby asked that the bridge be blown up by the end of the first week in November, at the latest. For it was his intention to launch his attack against the Turks in southern Palestine on October 31st.

MEDITERRANEAN SEA

BEIRUT

● Baalbeck

● DAMASCUS

HAIFA

Sea of
Galilee

Deraa

Jaffa

Jordan River

Hejaz Railway

JERUSALEM

AMMAN

Asrak

Madeba

Gaza

Dead
Sea

Beersheba

Kerak

WADI SIRHAN

Tafila

Jurf

Shobeck

Maan

Abu el Lisaal

Guweira

Aqaba

Gulf of Aqaba

RED SEA

HEJAZ CAMPAIGN:
Middle phase

miles

0   20   80

HEJAZ RAILWAY

Lawrence's expedition left Aqaba on October 24th. It traveled by way of Azrak, gathering reinforcements as it went. On the night of November 6th, after a roundabout ride of more than 400 miles, they crossed the Hejaz railroad south of Deraa. They made their way carefully, choosing a stony part of the desert where no marks of camel hoofs would betray signs of their passing. Not far beyond the Hejaz railroad they found a deep pit where they lay low for the whole of the next day, unseen by passing patrols of the enemy.

To execute their assignment, Lawrence and his men would have to start from their hiding place after nightfall, reach the Yarmuk gorge, blow up the railroad and be back across the Hejaz line before dawn. This meant an eighty-mile ride in the darkness over largely unknown country. Accordingly, Lawrence decided to leave a large part of his force behind, for only the finest mounts and the best riders could hope to achieve this almost impossible feat. Lawrence picked his men carefully and left shortly after sunset.

Despite stray shots fired by Arab tribesmen terrified by this shadowy band of soldiers riding through the darkness of the night, they remained unseen by the Turks. To the northeast they could see the white glare of the lights at Deraa station. Then, as the land began to slope downhill, they could hear the faint, faraway murmur of the Yarmuk River plunging down the gorge. As they grew nearer, the murmur gradually increased to a hollow roar. Lawrence knew they were drawing near to the great Tell el Shebab gorge, where their target bridge spanned the stream. Minutes later, moving down-river and now away from the roar of the falls, they found themselves on the edge of the ravine itself, staring down into the darkness.

There was the bridge, a shape blacker even than the blackness of the gorge. At the far end they could make out a white sheen and flickering points of light—the tents and fires of the Turkish guard. Slightly nearer, though still on the far end of the bridge, stood a solitary sentry.

Softly, silently, some carrying rifles, others armed with machine guns or carrying bags of blasting gelignite, Lawrence and the Arabs moved down into the darkness. From dangerous handhold to still more dangerous foothold they crept. Lawrence, in the lead as ever, had just reached the bridge. As he was climbing down to the girders beneath, one of the Arabs, in a desperate effort to keep from falling, dropped his gun. The metallic clatter of the rifle, striking from stone to stone, echoed through the silent gorge.

The Turkish sentry yelled a warning and the guards came racing out of their tents, their fingers already pressing on the triggers of their guns. Bullets whined in among Lawrence and his men, smashing into the rocks behind them, whistling off at all angles in screaming ricochet.

The fifteen men carrying the bags of gelignite took no chances of a direct hit on the deadly explosives they were carrying. They dropped their loads and fled for their lives. Panic developed among the others, and soon the whole party was racing back for their camels. Lawrence had no option but to follow them. And so what might have been his greatest triumph turned into his greatest failure—because one man had lost his grip on a rifle.

After a wild flight back they managed to re-cross the Hejaz railroad before dawn. The Arabs, their terror of the night departed, were now bitterly angry with themselves. They wanted revenge. They longed to carry out some exploit to justify their long trip north. Since they were close to the Hejaz railroad, the most obvious form of revenge was to blow up a Turkish train. Lawrence agreed, but reluctantly and much against his better judgment. He had already sent his machine-gunners back to Azrak. And he knew that attacking trains, most of which carried Turkish troops, could be very dangerous indeed without machine guns.

However, his better judgment notwithstanding, Lawrence set about digging a hole under the railroad line and installing an electrical mine. This type of explosive was fired by pressing down the plunger of an exploder, about sixty yards away, to which the mine was connected with wires. He had barely finished burying the explosive charge when a long train came by, the first ten wagons of which were packed full of Turkish troops. As the leading locomotive passed over the mine, Lawrence was only sixty yards away, behind a tiny bush which offered him neither protection nor concealment. Nevertheless, he pressed down on the plunger.

Nothing happened—an electrical fault. The train steamed slowly by, the troops gazing incuriously at the dirty little Arab squatting in the desert. Fortunately for Lawrence, his now famous white and gold robes were so stained and tarnished by his long journeyings as to be quite unrecognizable. Lawrence waved at them. The Turks ignored him completely. Had they but known that they were ignoring the most wanted man in all Arabia, a man with a price of £20,000 on his head . . .

Lawrence fixed the electrical fault in the detonator and waited patiently for the next train. This time there was no failure. The explosion was tremendous, far greater than even Lawrence—who was by this time a first-class expert in explosives—had expected.

The leading locomotive was blown almost to pieces. Great chunks of flying metal from the shattered engine were scattered far over the desert. A smaller piece broke one of Lawrence's toes while another sliced open his left arm. The body of the engineer crashed heavily to the ground just beside him. It had been flung almost sixty yards through the air by the terrific power of the explosion.

Half stunned, Lawrence tried to lurch away from the scene of the explosion. But the folly of attacking a train without machine guns was now apparent. For it turned out that this train had no fewer than 400 Turkish troops aboard, including a general who was on his way to take over command in Jerusalem. The Turks opened up a disciplined and concentrated fire on the Bedouin force. It was only by a near miracle, and at the expense of seven of his men who were wounded in their successful attempt to rescue him, that Lawrence escaped with his life. But he escaped far from scot-free. In addition to his broken toe, his gashed arm and the severe bruising caused by the flying debris from the exploding locomotive, he had been wounded five times by enemy bullets.

The Bedouins and their injured leader made their way slowly and wearily back to Azrak, which Lawrence had chosen for his winter headquarters. Beyond all doubt, this expedition to the north had been the biggest setback yet experienced by Lawrence in the Arab Revolt. But his greatest suffering and humiliation were yet to come.

Lying in his tent in Azrak and recovering from his wounds, Lawrence worked out the future course of his campaign. He decided that the next assault ought to be launched against the town of Deraa itself. Little was known about the defenses of Deraa, but it was rumored that there was a secret approach route into the town—a route unknown to the occupying Turks.

As soon as his wounds had healed, Lawrence decided to go to see for himself. He disguised himself as a Circassian, a member of a Caucasian people among whom were many with hair as fair and eyes as blue as Lawrence's own. Then, accompanied by only one friend, he made his way into enemy-held Deraa.

Unfortunately for Lawrence, many Circassians had migrated to Turkey after their area was conquered by Russia. And many of the Circassians had been impressed into the Turkish army much against their will. Even more unfortunately for Lawrence, many of those conscripts deserted just as promptly as possible. Lawrence was mistaken for one of those Circassian deserters by a Turkish sergeant in the streets of Deraa.

He was arrested on the spot, taken into a barracks, stripped and mercilessly flogged with a whip until he was beaten into unconsciousness. Then bleeding and half dead, he was taken into an ambulance room, where his wounds were roughly dressed. The last of the soldiers to leave, possibly an Arab sympathizer, told him that the door to the next room was not locked. Incredibly, for the second time in a few weeks, the Turks, with Lawrence in their power, had failed to identify him for the man he was.

Lawrence lay there all night, semiconscious and freezing cold. The next morning he pulled himself shakily to his feet and lurched into the adjacent room, where he found an old Arab robe. Donning it he escaped by a window. It was a tribute to Lawrence's amazing stamina that he was able to walk at all. He managed to make good his escape from Deraa and while doing so discovered the secret route into the town! Once again he made his way painfully back to his headquarters at Azrak.

But if things had been going badly for Lawrence, they had been going splendidly for Allenby. Launching his attack at the beginning of November, Allenby soon burst through the Gaza line and drove the Turks northward up through Palestine, finally taking Jerusalem itself.

Lawrence, soon after his bitter experience in Deraa, was summoned by Allenby to Palestine. He went by air and, to his great pleasure, was given a position of honor at the official entry into Jerusalem. This was, Lawrence afterward said, the greatest day of the war for him.

To his surprise and delight, Lawrence found Allenby in no way upset over the failure at the Yarmuk gorge. In Allenby's eyes it was impossible for Lawrence to have performed a greater service for him than pinning down the 25,000 Turkish troops to the east and south of the Dead Sea.

Allenby, more confident than ever of victory, was full of fresh plans. He intended to push north from Jerusalem, take Jericho and then clear the Jordan valley to the north of the Dead Sea. He asked that Feisal and Lawrence now move the main Arab forces north from Aqaba to the villages round Tafila, south and east of the Dead Sea. There they could link up with the British forces and also prevent the Turks from securing any further food supplies from the very rich corn belt in that area. Lawrence at once agreed and lost no time in returning to Aqaba.

In the depths of winter—and a very bitter winter it was to be, too—the Arabian army began its campaign against the Turks holding the invaluable corn belt. This belt ran more or less due north and parallel to the Hejaz railroad. It centered on four main towns: Shobek in the very south,

Tafila north of that, Kerak beyond that and finally, due east of the northern tip of the Dead Sea, Madeba.

But the first objective was none of those towns. It was the railroad station at Jurf. As the first step in the campaign, the capture of this station made good sense. With the line cut to the north and south and the station destroyed, the Turks would be unable to rush reinforcements to either Shobek or Tafila. These were the first two—and indeed the most important two—towns on the Arabs' list.

The Bedouins, under Nasir, moved in silently on Jurf during the hours of darkness. Taking up a position behind a high ridge overlooking the station, they cut the railroad line to the north and south. Then in the first light of dawn, the Arabs launched a headlong camel-back charge. The Turks collapsed completely before the Arabs' mad, yelling charge. Two hundred prisoners were taken and the station and two trains destroyed for the loss of only two Arab lives.

The cold now became intense and snow fell heavily during the next three days. The Arabs had only their tents as protection against this extreme weather, and in one day ten men died from exposure. But, cold or not the Arabs now had the bit in their teeth. A force operating farther to the west stormed and took Shobek. And a day or two later, after a desperate night ride through deep drifting snow and icy winds, Nasir, Lawrence, Auda and a small band of men arrived shortly before dawn on the edge of a cliff above Tafila.

They called upon the inhabitants and the Turkish garrison to surrender and were met instead by a storm of rifle fire. The Arabs were too few to take the town by force—there were at least 150 Turks in the Garrison. Just as it seemed that they might have to withdraw, Auda rode forward to the edge of the town and roared in his great voice, "Dogs, know ye not Auda?"

They knew him all right. It would have been hard to find a man in northern Arabia—either Arab or Turk—who did not know him. Terror-stricken, they surrendered without offering another shot in their own defense.

But, although Lawrence could not possibly have guessed it, the battle for Tafila had not yet begun. The Turkish general in that area was enraged at the loss of the town. He promptly sent against the Arabs a force consisting of three battalions, a cavalry company of over a hundred, two heavy howitzers and twenty-seven machine guns. The whole group was under a regular divisional commander. The weak Arab pickets guarding the outskirts of Tafila were soon swept aside, and the Turkish force advanced on the town itself.

The Arab commander in charge of the main body of Feisal's troops had taken up a defensive position behind, instead of in front of, the town. Lawrence, walking alone in the darkness through the deep snow lying on the icebound ground, soon discovered that the townspeople were completely terrified at the prospect of being left quite defenseless. They knew all too well the Turks' love of revenge, their habit of massacring every man, woman and child in any village suspected of giving help to the Bedouin.

Lawrence made use of this fear. He sent the villagers, many of whom had arms of one kind or another, to harass the enemy advance by constant sniping. Meanwhile he ordered some of his own men to take up position on a ridge lying in the main path of the enemy's advance on the town. (This ridge was one of two; another lay several hundred yards nearer the town.) Then he went to see the Arab commander to persuade him to bring his troops up in front of the town.

The actual process of the battle was complicated and confusing, but this was essentially what happened. Lawrence's men kept moving constantly about the farther ridge, to give the impression of much greater numbers than there actually were. Meanwhile Lawrence arranged for the Arabian mounted troops—on camel, horse and muleback—to move around the Turkish flank to the right, keeping under cover. He positioned the armed villagers on the left.

The Turks advanced steadily on Lawrence's men on the ridge, bringing heavy fire to bear. Lawrence ordered his men to retreat to the other ridge, the one nearer the town. On the way there he very carefully paced out the distance between the two ridges. Soon after the Bedouins had reached the shelter of the closer ridge, the Turks occupied the one the Arabs had just abandoned. There they set up their twenty-seven machine guns.

The Turkish commander now started to launch an all-out assault, but he was too late. Even as the enemy machine guns opened up, Lawrence's replied from the other ridge. Thanks to Lawrence's careful measuring, his gunners had the range almost to a yard. Within minutes, most of the Turks' machine guns were out of action. At this crucial moment the mounted Arab cavalry swept down from the right flank while the villagers closed in from the left. Lawrence and his men charged across the open plain and in minutes the battle was over. The Turks were not only defeated but completely routed.

The Turks lost all but 100 of their men (1,000 being dead or prisoner), all their machine guns and both howitzers. And all this cost the lives of only about twenty-five Arabs. Like all Lawrence's victories, it was bought at a very cheap price indeed in terms of the lives of his own men. Captain Liddell Hart, a highly regarded British authority on military tactics, regarded this battle, small-scale as it was, as a modern masterpiece. It was the only pitched battle Lawrence directed in the entire course of the war. And it showed that he could have been—and was—as fine a military commander in the ordinary sense as he was a guerrilla leader.

As a fitting postscript to this story, it should be recorded that Lawrence achieved another, if very minor victory, immediately afterward. He heard that Turkish food ships, with provisions for their army, were lying at anchor in the shallows just off the Dead Sea coast. In a swift and violent attack made like nearly all Bedouin attacks in the first light of dawn, Lawrence's mounted Arabs charged out into the sea. They overcame the sleeping sailors and soldier guards and sank the boats where they lay. For this action, Lawrence wrote a report to Cairo in which he solemnly recommended himself for the naval D.S.O.

He didn't get his naval D.S.O. But he did get the military D.S.O for his brilliant conduct of the Battle of Tafila.

CHAPTER 7

FORWARD AGAIN!

IT HAD BEEN LAWRENCE'S ORIGINAL INTENTION, as agreed with Allenby, to push north from Tafila and capture Kerak and Madeba. Thus the Turks would be deprived of the food supplies of the rest of the rich corn belt lying to the east of the Dead Sea. But this proved to be impossible because of the arctic weather.

The conditions in the high hills to the southeast of the Dead Sea were more what one might have expected to find in Greenland or Siberia than in a semitropical country like Arabia. The cold was truly intense. Storms of sleet and hail swept over the bare, rugged countryside. These were followed by icy winds and howling blizzards that piled up great drifts of snow and made movement almost hopeless.

The Arabs sat and shivered in what little protection was offered by tents and ramshackle huts. Accustomed to the great heat of the desert, they had no defense against this bitter cold.

Desperately short of food, many of them near starvation, they died in scores. One Arab leader, Maulud, a former Turkish regiment commander who had gone over to Feisal, was reckoned as a desert fighter second only to the great Auda himself. But Maulud lost no less than half of the entire force with which he was besieging Maan. The men died not from Turkish bullets but simply because they froze to death. Maulud had begged the British in Cairo for thick winter clothing for his troops in place of the thin summer drill they wore. But the quartermaster in charge of stores there had refused on the grounds that the Arabs were fighting in a tropical country!

An advance north was impossible because of the snow, lack of protective clothing and weakness from hunger. Besides, the spirit of the Arabs was now extremely low.

The men wished of nothing, dreamed of nothing but a quick return to the warmer climate of their own desert homes. If the Arabs were allowed to melt away, however, Lawrence would be unable to carry out his promises to Allenby. And that would mean the end of the Arab Revolt itself, and with it the end of the dream of Arabian independence.

For if this dream of Arabian independence were to come true, Lawrence knew that the Arabs must be in at the capture of Damascus, which only could come with the final defeat of the Turks.

Despite the promises of independence he had made to Feisal on behalf of his own country, Lawrence did not really trust his own country—or her French allies—to carry out their part of the bargain. He had already heard strong rumors of a secret agreement (which actually existed) between France and Britain. They planned to divide up Syria, Palestine and Mesopotamia among themselves after the war, ignoring the Arab claims to those places. And this, Lawrence was sure, would be exactly what would happen if the Arabian army were not there at the end of the war to press its claims. Whatever happened, the Arabs to the south and east of the Dead Sea must not be allowed to melt away.

The answer to this problem was the answer that had solved so many other problems in the desert—gold. Gold would pay weary, discontented men who had not been paid for weeks. Gold would buy the promise of their future support. And, above all, gold would buy the food, the warmth and the clothing that would enable them to survive the winter. The gold lay at Guweira, north of Aqaba, 300 miles away. With four other men, Lawrence set out from the Dead Sea hills to fetch it.

It was a desperate journey, a journey no man would ever have undertaken had there not been the most desperate need. Even the longest, the cruelest journey Lawrence had ever made in the blazing heat of summer had been little enough in comparison with this.

The wind was a whetted knife that sliced through thin robes and chilled the men to the bone. Great drifts of snow blocked their path; driving blizzards blinded them so that they often lost their way. Ice-cold streams had to be forded time and again. As often as not streams and stretches of water would be frozen over. On one of those occasions Lawrence, leading his camel across a frozen river, nearly drowned when the ice broke beneath him. But his camel came close enough for Lawrence to catch hold of it and drag himself to safety.

And so they went on, slipping, sliding, stumbling, falling. Soaked to the skin, they became numbed with the cold, the pain and the exhaustion. Some of Lawrence's companions wept, sure that they were dying and wishing only to be left to die in peace. But Lawrence drove them on, at times using force, for he knew that to stop in this shelterless gale-swept desert of snow and ice would be surely to die.

And once again, as happened so often in the past, Lawrence's tremendous will power brought him and his companions to safety. They reached Guweira, ate and rested briefly, collected £30,000 in gold and set off again. It says much for the force of Lawrence's personality, his magical gift for making men follow him, that he managed to persuade his companions to accompany him on the return journey. It proved no less a nightmare than the ride to Guweira.

Once back among the Dead Sea villages, Lawrence gave the money into the keeping of Prince Zeid, Feisal's youngest brother, who was in command of the Arabs in the area. Zeid was to give his chiefs enough money to pay for their tribesmen's immediate needs. But he was to hold back most of it to induce them to move north against the Turks as soon as the winter was over.

No man could have blamed Lawrence had he taken a well-earned rest. For months now he had ridden forty miles a day on his camel. Sleeplessness and hunger had been his constant companions. He had been wounded so many times that he had lost count of the number. He had wasted away till he was almost skeleton thin. That last terrible 600-mile-around ride, the Arabs thought, must have brought him to the point of utter exhaustion.

But the stamina, strength and will power of that amazing little Englishman were beyond all normal reckoning. Almost immediately after his return, although haggard, worn and still sorely in need of sleep, Lawrence was on camel-back again. This time he headed north along the eastern shores of the Dead Sea and east of the Jordan valley. The capture of the corn belt, the linking up with Allenby to the north of the Dead Sea were still the chief objectives in his mind. But before any advance could be undertaken, he had to make certain of the active help of the tribes along the route.

As with many of Lawrence's exploring and spying missions, little is known of this trip. But it is known that the local chiefs he met on his reconnaissance gave him every encouragement and promised to join the revolt when the moment came. Lawrence returned to his base in the Dead Sea hills well satisfied.

His satisfaction did not last long. He was met by a crushing blow. The gold he had entrusted to Zeid, the gold that was to secure the help of the Arab chiefs in the new campaign, was all gone. Zeid, too young to resist the pressure brought to bear on him by the tribal chiefs, had given it all away! The Arabs had their money and now they had no intention of doing anything, except possibly returning home.

For the first time ever, Lawrence was in complete despair. It may have been that his exhaustion, the sufferings of the past months, had been too great, but it seemed to him that all hope was now gone. The help he had promised Allenby could never come; the dream of Arab independence would remain no more than a dream.

Sadly, bitterly, he mounted his camel and rode off to Beersheba, then Allenby's headquarters, to offer his resignation to the British commander in chief.

But Allenby flatly refused to accept Lawrence's resignation. He regarded this latest setback as a trifle compared to the vast help Lawrence and the army under Feisal were giving him. Were they not pinning down to the east and south of the Dead Sea an increasingly large proportion of the total Turkish forces?

Although the Arabs in the hills to the south of the Dead Sea had lost the will to win, Allenby pointed out that the main body of Feisal's forces at Aqaba and Azrak was as full of fight as ever.

Allenby's faith in Lawrence remained completely unshaken. Evidence of this came shortly afterward when Lawrence was raised to the rank of colonel, a considerable promotion for a man who had entered the army not much more than three years earlier.

Allenby was full of his new plans, and Lawrence and Feisal's Arabs were to play an important part in them. The general proposed to advance slowly on his left up the Mediterranean before launching a full-scale attack to the north with the cooperation of the British navy. At the same time he intended to carry out an assault eastward from Jericho, which he had just captured, against Amman. Firstly he intended to use it as a base for an attack against Damascus. Secondly he wanted to cut off the 25,000 Turkish soldiers who were stretched out in a long line from Amman to Medina. He also planned that Feisal's Arab army should make an all-out attack on the important station of Maan. This he felt was being used as the Turks' chief base for the attacks being carried out by them from time to time in the Aqaba and Tafila areas.

Lawrence didn't want any part of those plans. He felt that Allenby, in making the plans, had relied too much on a map. And a map was no help at all in understanding the type of country that was actually there, and the quality of the soldiers who would be fighting in the area.

He was against the attack on Amman because he was sure it would fail. The British army, composed mostly of Britons and Indians, was unused to desert fighting; the Turks were not. The British army would have to bring its scanty supplies across large stretches of desert, while the large Turkish garrison in Amman could be heavily supplied by rail from Damascus. The Turks, as fine defensive fighters as any in the world, would be safe behind the heavy fortifications of Amman. It would be impossible for the British to haul heavy artillery across the desert from Jericho to Amman. And without big guns there was no way of breaching those walls.

More, Lawrence disagreed with Allenby on the choice of Amman as a base for a subsequent attack on Damascus. Azrak, at the northern end of the Wadi Sirhan, would be much better. Amman looked more suitable on a map, but that was as far as it went. Azrak was actually better, much better. Lawrence knew, for he had been to both places. Allenby had been to neither.

Nor did Lawrence approve of the frontal attack Feisal's army was to make upon Maan. The Arabs had never made a direct daylight frontal attack on any town. Such a move would sacrifice all the Arab advantages of speed, mobility and surprise. There was only one way to subdue Maan, Lawrence argued. That was to cut the railroad to the north and south, starve the garrison, force them to come out and then cut them to ribbons piecemeal.

Finally, he disapproved of the idea of cutting the line

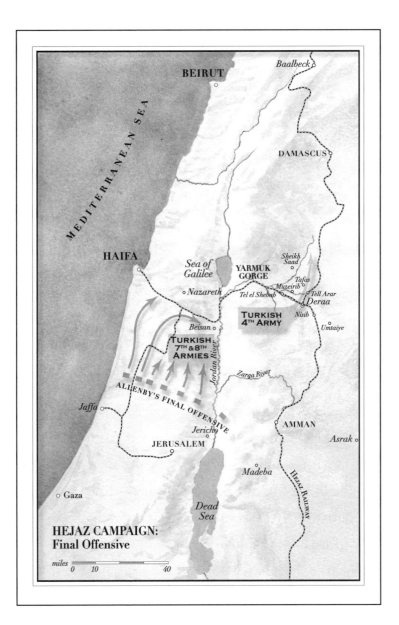

BEIRUT

Baalbeck

MEDITERRANEAN SEA

DAMASCUS

HAIFA

Sea of Galilee

YARMUK GORGE

Sheikh Saad

Tafas

Muzeirib

Tell Arar

Nazareth

Tel el Shebab

Deraa

TURKISH 4TH ARMY

Nisib

Umtaiye

Beisan

TURKISH 7TH & 8TH ARMIES

Jordan River

Zarga River

ALLENBY'S FINAL OFFENSIVE

Jaffa

AMMAN

Asrak

Jericho

JERUSALEM

Madeba

Gaza

Hejaz Railway

Dead Sea

HEJAZ CAMPAIGN:
Final Offensive

miles 0 10 40

completely and isolating the Turks to the south. This would certainly cut off the Turks in Medina. But at least 10,000, perhaps 15,000 men guarding the Hejaz railroad would then be forced to retreat north and join the main Turkish army.

Lawrence made all those objections, and he was overruled on every point. He was also to be proved right on every point. The two heavy British attacks on Amman failed completely. Farther south, the Arab attack against Maan had no more success. The Hejaz railroad, to Lawrence's secret relief, was not permanently destroyed. And Azrak, not Amman, became the main base east of the Dead Sea for further attacks against the Turks.

Had Allenby and his staff listened to Lawrence, many lives would have been spared and great quantities of supplies and ammunition saved. Even more important, the task of gathering in fresh tribes to join the Arab Revolt would not have been made so extremely difficult. For the northern tribes felt a considerable lack of confidence when they heard of the Turkish victories.

The British and Arab defeats took place in March, April and May of 1918. No further attacks were then made for the good reason that Allenby had been forced to call off his major campaign north into Palestine. In March, the Germans in Europe had launched a last, despairing all-out offensive against the French and British armies. So dangerous was this menace thought to be that a large part of Allenby's troops had been recalled to France to meet the grave threat. For the moment, Allenby's hands were tied. He could make no further move forward until fresh divisions arrived—and those had to come all the way from India.

But one bit of good fortune came out of this disappointment. Among the troops sent back to the Western Front was a brigade of the Imperial Camel Corps. Two thousand unwanted camels were going begging! Lawrence wasted no time. He asked for them—and he got them.

By June, Feisal and Lawrence were concentrating nearly all their forces at Azrak, Lawrence's original choice for a base. Auda was there too with the Howietat tribes, as well as the Emir of Ruwalla with the Ruwalla tribes. The Arab army had nearly all moved up from Aqaba, mounted on the camels left behind by the Imperial Camel Brigade. With them were two camel companies, each 300 strong, from the regular British army. Lawrence relates how astounded his Arabs were at the sight of those camel companies. Until now, the only Britons the Arab troops had ever seen had been an occasional commissioned or noncommissioned officer. They had not believed that there were so many Englishmen in the world.

Lawrence, by now, had regained all his old enthusiasm and confidence. If Allenby's hands were tied, his most certainly were not. Around him, in Azrak, he and Feisal had mustered as fine, as fast and as mobile a striking force as was to be found anywhere in the world at that time. How could they use this force?

There were no doubts in Lawrence's mind. The powerful Turkish garrisons at Amman and Azrak worried him not at all. They could be left to stew in their own juice as had happened with the garrison at Medina. As long ago as 1918 Lawrence had developed to an astonishing degree the modern blitzkrieg—lighting war—tactics of bypassing enemy strong points, leaving them to be mopped up later. These were the tactics with which the German panzer divisions so astonished the world when they burst through the Low Counties in the summer of 1940.

"Onward, ever onward" might well have been the motto of Lawrence of Arabia. The time had come to move and, as so often before, he turned his eyes to the north. This time he turned them toward Damascus.

CHAPTER 8

VICTORY ON ALL SIDES

DAMASCUS WAS THE HEART OF THE TURKS' ARABIAN empire. Regular British army officers scoffed at the idea that the Arab army could thread its way through the strong Turkish forces that lay to the north of Deraa and take Damascus by a surprise shock attack. But to Lawrence it was no wild dream. He was convinced it could be done. With typical imagination, daring and cold calculation he worked out to the slightest detail his plans for the secret approach to and storming of the city. Feisal was in complete and enthusiastic agreement with the scheme.

But first Lawrence had to have Allenby's approval. He met his commander in chief and was astonished to find that Allenby, who had received reinforcements much sooner than expected, was even then preparing for his big and final push against the Turks. Damascus would have to wait, Allenby said. When the big offensive started, Lawrence and the Arabs were to seize and hold the town of Deraa, the most important railroad junction in the Near East. This would not only prevent the Turks from bringing reinforcements from the north but would also cut off the escape route of a large part of the Turkish army in Palestine

Lawrence immediately agreed to shelve his own plans. He returned to join the Arab forces in Azrak, losing no time in making plans for his attack on Deraa.

In typical Lawrence fashion, the first thing he did was to convince the Turks that Deraa was the last place on earth he was thinking of attacking. He decided to deceive the Turks into thinking that his objective was the capture of Amman. This was a very natural thing for the Turks to think, as the British had twice made full-scale assaults on it in recent months.

An attempt by Lawrence to blow up the Kissir bridge near Amman aroused the fears of the Turks. And they were doubly anxious when they began to hear rumors that Lawrence was buying up all available barley in the area and ordering the delivery of great numbers of sheep to feed the Arabs who would be besieging Amman. It was Lawrence himself, of course, who was spreading the rumors. He also made sure that information was given to untrustworthy Arabs to the effect that Feisal's army was on the point of delivering a heavy attack on Amman from both east and west.

Alarmed, the Turks sent patrols to investigate and the patrols found plenty to worry them. Airfields were clearly marked out. There were crisscross tracks of many tires and large piles of empty food cans. (All this was the work of Lawrence himself with one armored car.) Then the Turks heard that a strong British and Arab force was actually operating to the southwest of Amman. (Lawrence had sent it there for the express purpose of strengthening the deception.) There were no longer any doubts in the minds of the enemy. Heavy reinforcements to meet this supposed major attack were swiftly brought down by rail from the north.

As a final masterstroke Lawrence intended, once the last of the Turkish reinforcements had poured into Amman from Deraa, to cut the railroad line just above Amman. Thus reinforcement could not pour out again when he launched his attack against Deraa.

As soon as Lawrence was ready, he sent the bulk of the Arab army north to its advance base for the attack on Deraa. This base was to be the village of Umtaiye, a place with excellent grazing and water for camels, only about fifteen miles southeast of Deraa itself. Lawrence intended to join the army as soon as his railroad demolition party brought him the news of the cutting of the railroad line above Amman.

But the news they brought him was that they had failed. Local tribesmen in the pay of the Turks had driven them off. These were grave tidings indeed; the whole success of his attack against Deraa depended on the Turks being unable to bring reinforcements up from Amman.

Never a man to waste a second or ask any person to engage on a dangerous enterprise if he himself were there to do it, Lawrence jumped into a Rolls-Royce car. It was "Crammed to the gunwales," as he said, "with gun-cotton and detonators." Escorted by two armored cars, he set off at high speed across the desert toward a bridge just north of Amman.

While the armored cars engaged—and finally overcame—the guard post at the bridge, Lawrence set the gun-cotton charges in the drainage holes in the curves of the arches. He then fixed the detonators and triggered off the explosion that shattered the bridge. It was the perfect type of demolition. It brought down the arches but left the pillars shakily standing, so that repair gangs would first have to complete the work of blowing up the pillars before they could begin to rebuild.

Lawrence was given no time at all to admire his handiwork. Even as the dust from the explosion cleared, heavy enemy patrols were seen approaching. Quickly the wreckers climbed into their vehicles and drove off. But Lawrence's Rolls-Royce had gone less than a quarter of a mile when a particularly bad bump broke one of the springs of his car. It was the first such accident Lawrence had ever had, and it couldn't have happened at a worse time. But he and his experienced desert fighters were equal to any emergency. Swiftly they found a length of wood, "sawed" it off to the right length with a burst of machine-gun fire, jammed it in place above the broken spring and made good their escape.

The next day found Lawrence and a detachment from his Arab forces astride the Hejaz railroad line at a place called Tell Arar, four miles to the north of Deraa. Lawrence, after much thought, had decided against an all-out attack on Deraa itself. He believed that without proper artillery and bomber support Feisal's Arabs could not take the heavily defended town without suffering far too many casualties. Even more important, Lawrence was by no means certain that Allenby's offensive would succeed. If Feisal and Lawrence took Deraa but Allenby failed, Lawrence knew that the Turks would spare no effort to recapture Deraa. And if they did that, Lawrence was only too keenly aware that they would massacre the Arab townsfolk, their usual practice when they recaptured an Arab town.

Lawrence, of course, had promised Allenby that he would take Deraa. But the purpose of that had been to block all railroad movement to the north, south and west of the town. The same effect could be achieved by destroying the railroad lines north, south and west of the town itself. Tell Arar on the northern line was chosen first.

The Turkish guard post there was quickly overcome. Lawrence's party then swiftly set about destroying ten miles of line—ten miles! It would take the Turks a long time to replace that. The wreckers used what were called "tulips" –small explosive charges placed every thirty feet or so along the line under the hollow ties. The explosions blew the ties about two feet above the ground, lifting the rails with them, drawing them together and shortening them, leaving a gap of several inches between each set of rails. It did not look spectacular, but it was the most effective way of destroying a railroad and by far the most difficult to repair.

As they were working they were attacked with both bombs and machine-gun fire by eight Turkish airplanes. The Arabs scattered, with few casualties, but the attack held up their work. Suddenly, there appeared the Arab army's sole surviving aircraft, an ancient and battered machine not much better than the one the Wright brothers had flown at Kitty Hawk. It's pilot was successful in drawing off the Turkish planes. He soon reappeared, however, with several enemy planes in closer pursuit and was forced to crash-land in the desert. The pilot, a Lieutenant Junor, was a man very much after Lawrence's own heart. He jumped from the wreck and wrenched free his machine gun. Mounting it on a borrowed Ford, he set off to carry on his own private war against the Turks!

When the railroad at Tell Arar had been thoroughly destroyed, Lawrence and his men rode off to destroy the west line, the vital one carrying the supplies to the main Turkish army in Palestine. Their objective was the station of Muzeirib, about five miles to the west of Deraa. On the way, they were attacked by Turkish bombers. Lawrence was wounded in the arm by shrapnel, but he kept going. The station garrison collapsed under the first fierce Arab attack, and the Bedouins then set about their methodical task of blowing up the line on both sides of the station. While they were engaged in this, Lawrence took great pleasure in personally cutting the telegraph line to the headquarters of the Turkish army in Palestine.

Lawrence then conceived the idea of moving still farther west, deep into the Yarmuk gorge, and blowing up the great Tell el Shebab bridge, where he had failed the previous November. When he arrived there, however, he found it heavily guarded by Germans, so he had to abandon the idea. But Lawrence was satisfied. This meant that the Turks in Palestine were being forced to pull out German soldiers—their very best troops—to meet the threat of his guerrilla tactics.

The only line now left to cut was the one leading south from Deraa. Lawrence chose as his point of attack a heavily built stone bridge over a valley closer to the station of Nisib, ten miles south of Deraa. A swift cross-country ride and they were there. The main body of the Arabs launched an attack against the heavily defended station itself. Meanwhile Lawrence and a small band advanced on the bridge under cover of this diversion.

There was no means of telling whether the bridge was still under guard or whether the soldiers there had rushed back to help the Nisib garrison. The only way to find out was to walk down into the valley and see.

For the first time—and last—time in the whole Arabian campaign, Lawrence's men refused to follow him. And the men with him were the specially picked, battle-hardened men of his own bodyguard. They had been riding and wrecking and fighting continuously for four days without any sleep at all and with scarcely any food. Having reached the point of complete and utter exhaustion, they felt they could go no farther. What may have influenced their refusal was the fact that they did not relish the prospect— and who can blame them?—of carrying nearly 700 pounds of blasting gelatin down the exposed slopes to the bridge. For a burst of fire from the defenders of the bridge—if any guards were still there—could blow them all to pieces if a stay bullet should hit one of the bags of gelatin.

Lawrence tried his hardest, both by persuasion and by joking, to make the men accompany him, but all to no purpose. After a short time he gave up. Gray-faced, wounded, his features lined with the strains of sleeplessness and exhaustion, he turned and left them. Quite alone, ignoring the bullets flying all around him, he trudged on wearily down the bridge.

His bodyguard watched him go, plodding on slowly to the bridge. Then finally, after a long wait, they struggled to their feet and followed him. Shame may have been the reason, or the vast affection and respect in which they all held this little Englishman. Or it may have been the certain knowledge of what would happen if El Aurens, as they called him, died alone in front of the enemy while his bodyguard lay cowering in a place of safety. There would be no place left in all Arabia where they could hide, where the vengeance of Feisal and his Arabs would not seek them out.

The bridge was deserted; the defenders had fled. The high explosives were placed against the supports of the bridge and the fuses set. Lawrence waved back the others and touched off the fuses himself. There came the deep muffled boom of an explosion. Then the whole great stone mass of the bridge collapsed and rumbled down heavily into the valley below.

This was the last bridge ever blown up by Lawrence of Arabia. In the course of the desert war he himself had destroyed no fewer than seventy-nine railroad bridges.

Deraa was now isolated, completely cut off on all sides. The movement of Turkish troops, supplies and ammunition north, south or west had become completely impossible. Magnificently, indeed, had Lawrence carried out his promised share of the offensive against the Turks.

And just as magnificently was Allenby to carry out his promised—and greater—share of the big push. Only a few hours after the Nisib bridge had crashed into the valley, he sent the massed waves of his troops crashing solidly into the Turkish defenses in Palestine.

Lawrence, before moving on Deraa, had convinced the Turks that his true objective was Amman. And he had fooled them into concentrating their troops there. In the same way Allenby had set about convincing the enemy that his objective was far from where he actually intended to launch his offensive. And he too was spectacularly successful in making them concentrate their forces in the wrong place.

Allenby's line was stretched out from the Mediterranean Sea to the east of the valley of the Jordan. His intention was to launch his heaviest attack on the west, in the coastal area. So he set about convincing the Turks that the attack was coming in the Jericho-Amman sector in the east.

Day after day Turkish reconnaissance planes could see vast dust clouds moving slowly eastward. There was no doubt in the Turks' minds that these were caused by battalions of infantry marching to build up the strength on Allenby's right wing. The dust clouds, in fact, were caused by brushwood sledges being dragged across the plain by donkeys. In rainy weather, when the dust was laid, the Turkish pilots could see and photograph actual columns of troops marching steadily east. The pilots must have marveled at their freedom from attack by British planes. They did not know it was Allenby's desire that they should observe as much as possible.

What the Turks also didn't know, of course, was that as soon as darkness fell the troops, mules and sledges were loaded in trucks. Then they were driven back to the west again to begin the same march eastward next day.

Great camps were set up in the east. When the Turkish planes came over, a few men dashing busily around could give quite an air of activity to the rows of tents. They could convince the Turks that for every man visible there would be 100 under canvas sheltering from the heat of the sun or the wetness of the rain, as the case might be. Actually, the few men they saw were all the men who were there.

It was Allenby's intention that the main shock of the

attack should be carried by his cavalry. Every night another squadron or two of cavalry would ride over to hidden positions on the west. But canvas dummies of horses were placed in their old quarters to reassure the enemy observers that the cavalry was still in the east. And so it went on until a day or two before the assault there were 15,000 canvas dummies of horses concentrated in the Jericho area! So perfect was the deception that it didn't matter when an Indian deserter from the British forces told the Turks Allenby's true plans. General Liman von Sanders, the German commander in chief of all the Turkish and German forces in Palestine, flatly refused to believe him.

The surprise of the attack, when it came at dawn on the nineteenth of September, was complete. Allenby began by making a small-scale attack on the right, which was exactly what the Turks had expected. They sent out a hurried call for more reinforcements to be sent east.

Then 400 heavy guns on the west, near the coast, opened up in an intense artillery barrage of the Turkish defensive positions. Before the dazed Turks in their thinly held trenches had time to recover from the shock and sheer weight of this violent barrage, British and Indian infantrymen were on them like a storm. The attackers completely crushed all defenses and then wheeled inland to roll over one Turkish strong point after another.

Meanwhile the cavalry had burst through on the coast and raced due north for thirty miles before breaking inland. One force made for and captured the Turkish head-quarters town of Nazareth, from which Liman von Sanders and his staff, stupefied by this incredible turn of events, barely managed to escape. Another force, curving slightly to the south, cut across the only railroad out of Palestine and reached Beisan in the Jordan Valley, so blocking off all escape to the north.

The only chance of escape now left was to the east, across the River Jordan. But even here no hope remained for the dazed and luckless Turks. The escape routes lay through winding gorges leading down to the river. And in those narrow defiles the fleeing troops were caught by British planes and bombed and machine-gunned into complete confusion and surrender. The rout and destruction of the Turkish forces in Palestine were now complete.

Before Allenby's assault, Liman von Sanders had had under his command three separate armies. There were the Seventh and Eighth Armies to the west of the Jordan and—the most powerful of the three—the Fourth Army, to the east of the Jordan. In one brief and disastrous blow both his Seventh and Eighth Armies had been utterly destroyed. Only the Fourth Army, lying between the Jordan and the Hejaz railroad, was still intact.

If this army remained where it was, Liman von Sanders knew that it wouldn't remain intact long. After taking a few days to regroup his forces, Allenby would be launching another hammer-blow attack across the Jordan. The only hope for the Turkish Fourth Army lay in an immediate retreat to Damascus and the north.

But squarely across the line of this retreat lay Lawrence and his waiting Arabs.

CHAPTER 9

THE ROUT OF THE TURKS

LAWRENCE AND FEISAL'S ARABS, ENCAMPED ON
the outskirts of Deraa, were finding the waiting very hard
indeed. Since Lieutenant Junor's ancient plane had
crashed a few days previously, the Arab army had had no
air protection whatsoever. The Turks had brought some
more German-built airplanes into the area and were flying
them nonstop against the defenseless Arabs, whose rifles
were quite useless as protection. So constant were the air
attacks, so ruthlessly did the German pilots press home
their bombing and machine-gun raids that a very real

danger developed. The Arab army might have to withdraw deep into the desert, beyond the range of the enemy planes. And if they were forced to do this, then there would be no one left to block the northward retreat of the Turkish Fourth Army.

It was a time for desperate measures. Lawrence determined to make an attack on an enemy airfield. Fittingly enough, the companion he chose for this exploit was Junor, the pilot who no longer had a plane.

They approached the Turkish airfield in two fast armored cars, cutting off the engines some distance away and coasting silently up to the edge of the field. Three Turkish planes were on the ground. Just as Lawrence and Junor accelerated their cars to dash in among the planes, they found their way blocked by a deep ditch. They halted, shot one of the planes to pieces with 1,500 rounds of continuous machine-gun fire, then turned and fled for their lives. They had to. The other planes, beyond the reach of their machine guns, had already taken off and were closing in to take revenge. For endless minutes the strange fight continued. The planes bombed and machine-gunned the cars as they twisted and wove their way across the stony desert. Lawrence was gashed in the hand by a flying stone and had the front tire of his car blown off by a bomb. But both men managed to escape.

One plane destroyed wasn't going to make much difference, Lawrence realized. And the Turks would put heavy guards on their landing fields to see that no such raid could happen again. The only answer was to get British fighter planes, and get them without delay. He drove down to Azrak, flew to Palestine and heard for the first time of Allenby's overwhelming success against the Turkish Seventh and Eighth Armies. He managed to talk Allenby into giving him two Bristols—modern twin-seat fighters, more than a match for anything the enemy had—plus a big Handley Page bomber to carry gasoline and spares.

Even so small an item as those two fighters made a tremendous difference in the Deraa area. After two Turkish planes had been shot down in flames and three others had been badly damaged, the enemy planes ceased almost completely to be a menace to Feisal's Arabs.

Just as welcome as the planes which Lawrence secured for Feisal's troops was the great news of the Turkish collapse in Palestine. By way of celebration the Arabs finally smashed the Hejaz railroad so thoroughly and completely that it could no longer be used at all by the Turks. Thus they made sure that none of the many thousands of Turkish troops in the south could come north to help the retreating Fourth Army.

That same day other Arabs, under the Emir of Ruwalla and Tallal, a chieftain from a village to the north of Deraa, came into contact for the first time with units of the retreating Turkish Fourth Army. They took several hundred prisoners.

It was obvious to Lawrence that the Fourth Army was retreating to Damascus. It was equally obvious that the main body of that retreating army would have to go by one of two routes. They could go through Deraa and up the railroad line, or they could travel by what was known as the Pilgrims' Road. This ran northward through Muzeirib—the station to the west of Deraa where Lawrence had recently cut the Palestine railroad. Some miles north of Deraa, near the village of Sheik Saad, these two escape routes came close together. With typical daring, Lawrence proposed that the main body of the Arab army should move north to this area and lie in wait for the Turks.

His plan met with very strong opposition, especially from a senior British officer. The latter was convinced that to plant the Arab force in the escape route of an enemy who outnumbered them twenty to one would just be inviting wholesale massacre. Lawrence pointed out the advantages: good grazing with plenty of water, high country which gave them first-class observation all around, and a means of retreat to the west or north should the need arise. He was also convinced that the Fourth Army, though greatly outnumbering them, would be thoroughly disorganized. Thus the Turks would be unable to bring a fraction of their total power to bear at any one point.

What Lawrence did not say, but what was almost certainly in his mind, was that he was eager to have the Arabs as far north as possible. The British had promised him—although in his heart he no longer believed them—that what the Arabs took they should have when peace came. And the eyes and heart of every Arab were set on Damascus. Lawrence intended that the Arabs should get there before the British—and Sheik Saad was well on the way.

Eventually Lawrence overruled all objections, and the

move northwest from their base at Umtaiye began. Auda and Tallal—the latter now very anxious for the welfare of his village in the Sheik Saad area—were in the lead. On the way several hundred prisoners were taken, a train was destroyed, and much booty was captured.

They traveled overnight, arriving at their destination by dawn on September 27th. No sooner were they in position than a German and Austrian machine-gun company, heading northward through what they took to be deserted country, blundered straight into their waiting arms. The Arabs captured them to a man.

From the vantage point of a high hill near Sheik Saad, Lawrence and his men could see many different detachments of Turkish troops moving northward. The Turks, having received during the night false reports saying that a huge Arab army had moved to the north, were busily evacuating Deraa. Foolishly they had burned the only six remaining airplanes in the town. By doing this, they had destroyed the only "eyes" that could have given them a true report as to the position and number of the Arabs.

From his commanding position on the hill, Lawrence

sent bands of Arabs to waylay and cut off various bodies of Turkish troops. These troops, as Lawrence had so accurately forecast, were retreating in disorder and not as an organized army. In the first day alone, the Arabs captured no fewer than 2,000 Turks.

A British airplane flew over Lawrence's position and dropped a note which said that two really large enemy columns were approaching from the south. One, between 6,000 and 7,000 strong, was marching up from Deraa while the other, about 2,000 strong, was coming up the Pilgrims' Road from Muzeirib. Lawrence had hoped that the main body of Allenby's cavalry might move northeastward from the Jordan in time to intercept such large forces. But apparently it had been delayed. At that moment, Lawrence had only 600 men to deal with the Turks' 9,000.

Lawrence didn't hesitate. The larger column was much too big for him even to think of making a daylight attack on it. Instead, he sent off a small band of mounted Arabs to harass and snipe at the Turks from ambush and do all in their power to delay the enemy force. He would deal with them during the darkness of the night.

But the 2,000-strong force was a different matter. Not only did he think that his outnumbered Arabs were more than a match for these Turks, but it was essential that his men intercept them as soon as possible. Tallal's own village of Tafas lay directly in the line of retreat of this smaller column. And already fearful tales were beginning to come in about the grim massacres wrought by the Turks in the Arab villages through which they passed in retreat.

But the Arabs and their camels and horses were exhausted from the endless riding and fighting. No one had had any sleep for three nights. Despite Tallal's desperate anxiety they made slow progress—fatally slow progress, for they arrived at Tafas too late. The Turks had reached the village an hour previously and were already leaving.

The township of Tafas, the village over which Tallal had ruled so long, was no longer a village. It was a blackened, smoking grave, inhabited only by the dead. The dead lay everywhere—old men, women, children, even the smallest babies, all ruthlessly massacred by the Turks.

Tallal, Lawrence relates, gave a moan like a hurt animal.

Then he rode off to higher ground and remained there for some moments, shivering violently and staring after the retreating Turks. Lawrence moved to speak to him, but Auda caught his rein and stopped him. In one blow, in one moment, Tallal had lost every person in the world who mattered to him. And the older Auda, wiser in this matter than Lawrence, realized that Tallal now had nothing left to live for.

Slowly Tallal drew his headcloth about his face. Then he suddenly thrust his spurs into the sides of his horse and galloped headlong straight into the main body of the enemy.

Both sides stopped shooting. Lawrence and his men remained as motionless as stones while Tallal galloped madly toward the Turks. The drumming of his horse's hoofbeats sounded unnaturally loud in the strange and sudden silence. Then he stood high in the saddle and shouted out, "Tallal, Tallal," twice in a great voice. "Instantly," Lawrence recounts, "their rifles and machine-guns crashed out, and he and his mare, riddled through and through with bullets, fell dead among the lance points."

"God give him mercy," Auda said softly. "We will take his price."

And Auda, the greatest and most feared desert fighter of his time, was as good as his word. The outnumbered Arabs, driven into a madness of rage and hate by the grim horor of Tafas, fell upon the Turks like a pack of starving wolves. Brilliantly led by an Auda who remained ice-cold in his terrible anger, they drove the Turkish column into wild country. There they split them up and began to destroy them piecemeal. The Turks broke and ran, completely terror-stricken, for they could see that now there was no hope, no escape, no life. The Arabs were taking no prisoners. The captured, the wounded, those who surrendered—all went to their death under the knife, the lance, the gun.

Only one detachment of the Turkish forces fought back well. This one formation of German and Austrian machine-gunners conducted themselves magnificently and fought back with splendid gallantry and courage. Even Lawrence, after the horror of Tafas and with the knowledge that the Germans had killed two of his brothers on the Western Front, could hardly find words to express his admiration for them. But even those brave men could not last forever.

There was a blood-madness on the Bedouins that evening. Even had he wished to—and he didn't—Lawrence could no longer have stopped the killing. Once they came across a 200-strong group of Turkish prisoners in the charge of some Arabs who had not heard of Tafas. Beside them lay on the ground a wounded and dying Arab, pinned immovably to the earth by Turkish bayonets. When asked who had done this, the dying man nodded silently toward the prisoners. For a few seconds and a few seconds only, the crash of machine-gun fire and rifles rolled across the darkening desert. Then Lawrence and his Arabs rode on, leaving 200 dead behind them. Today it all sounds inhuman and barbaric. But the Arabs had suffered for many years under the rule of the Turks. And the sight of the slaughter at Tafas had roused them to a fevered pitch. Moreover, the Bedouin tribesmen were accustomed to carrying on blood feuds with their enemies.

The killing went on until the entire Turkish force of 2,000 had died. But still the Arab thirst for vengeance was unslaked. They rode madly across country, through a dark cold night with a great gale blowing from the southeast, and fell upon the 7,000-strong Turkish column that had been marching north from Deraa. Auda, as ever, was in the lead, directing the running fight. Like gray rushing ghosts in the wind-filled blackness of the night, his men were slicing their way through the stumbling, exhausted, panic-stricken Turks. Auda sent them to kill swiftly and silently and terribly and then ride clear to kill again. He sent them to cut off and annihilate stray wandering groups of soldiers, to set up cunningly concealed ambushes and wipe out scores of unsuspecting soldiery in a moment. Backing up Auda was the Emir of Ruwalla with his men. Together they took a terrible toll of the Turks. By dawn, barely 2,000 of that great column still survived

Sickened at last by the slaughter, and bone-tired after four consecutive nights in the saddle, Lawrence turned his camel and raced madly back to Deraa. "A crazy ride," he said later, "through a country of murder and night terror." But Lawrence had reason for his haste. A force of Arabs, under Sherif Nasir, overcoming the last feeble tokens of Turkish resistance, had already entered Deraa. And Lawrence was ever mindful of the British promises earlier in the war that what the Arabs should take they should have. He wanted to see the town under firmly responsible Arab control before the approaching British Fourth Cavalry Division, under a General Barrow, could move in and claim it for their own.

Swiftly Lawrence helped Nasir arrange for a military governor, police and guards for the water pumps, engine sheds and stores. Work was also started on repairing the station and railroad lines. When General Barrow finally did arrive—his troops spread out and ready to encircle and attack the town—Lawrence was there to meet him. He gave Barrow the unwelcome news that Deraa was completely in Arab hands and that they were more than capable of running it themselves. There was little Barrow could do, short of using force, and there was nothing in his orders about attacking Britain's Arab allies!

Lawrence did not remain long in Deraa. It had been essential that the British lose the race into Deraa, but it was even more important that the Arab forces be the first through the gates of Damascus.

CHAPTER 10

A TRIUMPHANT ENTRY INTO DAMASCUS

LAWRENCE WAITED LONG ENOUGH TO HAND OVER the town of Deraa to Prince Faisal, who had just arrived from Azrak. Then he set off before dawn in his stripped-down Rolls-Royce—his favorite desert vehicle, which he had christened "Blue Mist." Accompanied by another British officer, he set out to cover the sixty-odd miles to Damascus. Before he had gone very far, he was held up by General Barrow's cavalry, which had left some hours earlier. But this did not stop Lawrence for long. He turned Blue Mist off the road, climbed up the embankment of the

Hejaz railroad and bumped along the track until he had bypassed the cavalry. Then he took to the road again.

Toward evening, some ten miles south of Damascus, they heard the sound of heavy firing and came within sight of a column of 2,000 Turkish troops. These were the survivors of the Turkish force of 7,000 which Auda and the Emir of Ruwalla had handled so roughly. Auda and Ruwalla, along with Nasir, were still there, circling the troops on camel and horseback, slowing down the column's retreat and gradually, patiently, whittling down its numbers.

George Barrow had asked Nasir and Auda to guard his right flank as he rode north. But those old desert warriors knew only too well what Feisal and Lawrence had in mind. They had no intention of allowing Barrow into Damascus before them. Barrow now lay far behind.

Nevertheless, Lawrence saw that it would be necessary to ask Barrow—or the advance guard of his cavalry—for some assistance for the greatly outnumbered Arabs. Otherwise the Turks might escape north of Damascus when dark fell. He asked Nasir to try to hold up the Turks for an hour. Then he raced back in his Rolls and persuaded a brigade commander to send forward a horse battery and cavalry regiment.

Darkness was falling when the British guns came into range. As the first shells crashed among them, the weary and dispirited Turks abandoned their guns and transport and made quickly for the refuge offered by the heights of a nearby hill. But there was no refuge waiting on that hill —only the tireless Auda and his men. The Arab leader had cunningly placed his men there in anticipation of this very move. By now even Auda was tired of blood and slaughter. That night he killed only when he had to, taking more than 600 prisoners. The few leaderless and terrified groups of men who managed to escape in the dark were easily captured during the next day or two. So was destroyed the last of the core of the Turkish Fourth Army.

Many men, both military critics and biographers, have made little of Lawrence's achievements, dismissing them as being of little value. Lawrence possessed a brilliantly original mind. He had a contempt for and an openly expressed impatience with the hidebound military mind of the day. Thus he was a man who made many enemies, both in life and in death. And Lawrence played into his critics' hands by offhandedly referring to the Arabian campaign as "the sideshow of a sideshow."

Much more fitting would be an adaptation of Churchill's words in describing the handful of World War II British fighter pilots who destroyed the German Luftwaffe in the Battle of Britain. "Never have so many owed so much to so few." As a sideshow, the Arabian campaign must be rated as one of the most remarkable in military history.

At no time during the war did Lawrence have a force of more than 3,000 Arabs. And nearly all his victories were achieved by a hard expeditionary core of about 600 men. It was chiefly with this tiny body of men that he destroyed the Turkish Fourth Army, killing about 6,000, wounding unknown numbers and taking more than 8,000 prisoners. In addition, during the last year of the war, this tiny force kept up its nonstop raiding attacks on Turkish garrisons and outposts and paralyzing cuts of railroad communications. It was responsible for keeping huge Turkish forces pinned down to the east and south of the Dead Sea. The Turks never knew in what place, from which direction the Arabs would attack next out of the desert dawn. So they were forced to pour more and more reinforcements into garrisons and outposts and along the Hejaz railroad as far south as Medina. Thus in 1918 rather more than 55,000 Turkish troops—*just over half of the entire Turkish forces south of Damascus*—were immobilized. And they were immobilized by this tiny will-o'-the wisp flying column of Arabian irregulars.

With his 600 men, Lawrence reduced by half the numbers of Turks Allenby had to face when he made his final offensive. And it is worth noting that Allenby did not make his move until he had no fewer than a quarter of a million men under his command.

At midnight Lawrence lay down in his blanket outside the gates of Damascus. Sleep would not come, partly because of the knowledge that his troops had reached the end of the road with victory now in sight, and partly because of the continuous rumble of heavy explosions and the bright red glare in the sky above Damascus. Lawrence was convinced that the Turks were burning and destroying the city rather than let it fall at last into the hands of the Arabs. But his fears and anxieties were needless. The explosions and fires were caused by German engineers blowing up ammunition and store dumps in the wake of the retreating Turkish garrison. The next morning Lawrence saw that Damascus, far from being destroyed, shimmered like a pearl in the morning sun.

Sherif Nasir and the Emir of Ruwalla had fought long and determinedly for the Arab cause. So Lawrence gave the two chiefs the honor of being the first to enter the city of Damascus on the first day of October, 1918. As always, Lawrence had an underlying reason for this. Had he himself made the first entry, the British might have claimed the town as their own on the ground that a senior British officer—Lawrence was now a colonel—had been the first through the gates.

When Lawrence finally drove into Damascus in his Rolls-Royce, he received a tremendous welcome. The crowds of liberated Arabs variously hailed him as El Aurens, Aurens Bey, Lurens Bey and Emir Dinamite. But he did not pause to savor the great pleasure of the moment. There was work to be done—13,000 Turkish soldiers in barracks and hospitals to be captured and cared for and a government to be formed. And order had to be restored to the city before the British made their appearance. It was Deraa all over again, but this time on a much vaster scale. If the British authorities found that the Arabs were incapable of restoring order and running the city, they would have every excuse for taking it over themselves.

Lawrence found Sherif Nasir and the Emir of Ruwalla at the town hall. There, too, he found Auda, the greatest warrior of them all. Auda was still fighting, this time with a fellow chieftain with whom he had had a violent disagreement. They dragged Auda off the unfortunate man who had then to be sent out of the city for his own safety.

More dismaying, Lawrence found at the town hall two Algerian brothers, Abd el Kader and Mohammed Said, who were strong Turkish supporters. Both of them were trying hard to convince Sherif Nasir, Feisal's chief Arab representative, that Mohammed Said was the only man for the position of the new governor of Damascus.

Lawrence was aghast. This pro-Turkish rabble-rouser would certainly make no attempt to get the affairs of Damascus running smoothly again. If the British arrived and found that the Arabs had allowed him to take over the city, they would certainly depose him and elect a more suitable man. This would mean, in effect, that it would be the British and not the Arabs who would control the city. And, as far as Lawrence could see, Sherif Nasir, a fine man but completely inexperienced in those political matters, was in danger of yielding to Mohammed Said's persuasions.

Lawrence took the matter into his own hands, and at once. He had already decided that a certain Shukri Pasha, a leading and respected citizen, as responsible and moderate in every way as the Algerian brothers were not, was the ideal choice for governor. Without delay and without consulting anyone, Lawrence took Shukri with him in his Rolls-Royce and made a ceremonial tour of Damascus. He informed the people that Shukri was to be the new governor of the city. It was more than just a ceremonial tour, it was a completely triumphal one; everywhere they were met with the most overwhelming enthusiasm.

Damascus went mad with joy. The men, Lawrence reported, tossed up their tarbooshes to cheer, and women tore off their veils. Householders threw flowers, curtains and carpets into the road before the car, while their wives splashed Lawrence and Shukri with bath-dippers of scent.

Dancing dervishes cut themselves in their mad frenzy, and, over and above the ceaseless clamor, came the steady chanting of "Feisal, Nasir, Shukri, Aurens." Shukri himself was more than popular with the Damascenes. And when they saw him in the company of the legendary Colonel Lawrence, the quarter of a million inhabitants of Damascus gave him their wholehearted approval as their choice of governor.

Satisfied that he knew the mood and the overwhelming desire of the people, Lawrence returned to the town hall and asked for the Algerian brothers to appear before him. He received the insolent reply that they were sleeping and not to be disturbed.

Lawrence immediately sent a messenger to say that if they did not come at once he would send British troops to fetch them. This was a double bluff. British troops were the last people Lawrence wished to see in Damascus at that moment. Lawrence was bluffing partly to bring the Algerians to their senses and partly for the benefit of the Emir of Ruwalla, who was standing by his side. The Emir asked Lawrence if the English were likely to come and Lawrence said, "Certainly: but the sorrow is that afterwards they may not go." The Emir, knowing all too well what Lawrence meant, told him the English were unnecessary and grimly promised him the full support of his Ruwalla tribesmen.

Before long the Algerian brothers appeared, accompanied by a strong bodyguard and intent on trouble. But suddenly they were no longer so keen on a showdown of violence when they saw Lawrence. For he had the Emir on one side and the feared Auda on the other and was flanked by the fierce desert tribesmen.

Lawrence, mincing no words, informed the Algerian brothers that their self-appointed government was dissolved on the spot and that Shukri was the new governor. Mohammed Said called Lawrence a great number of unpleasant names. Lawrence ignored him. Then Abd el Kader burst into a torrent of mad curses which Lawrence again ignored, this time in so contemptuous a manner that Abd el Kader drew his dagger to spring at him. Fast though he was, he was slow compared to Auda. But Abd el Kader was lucky; bystanders managed to drag Auda off before the old warrior could kill him. The Algerian brothers left in a hurry.

The question of the governorship settled, Lawrence turned his attention to the restoring of order in the city. First—and most necessary of all—he formed a police force. Secondly, he restored the water supply and the electrical services from the power stations. After that, gangs of street cleaners and scavengers were set up to clear away the appalling mess left behind by the Turks. For there was a very real danger of pestilence breaking out.

Then came the formation of fire brigades, the cleaning up of long neglected hospitals, the bringing in of desperately needed food from abandoned Turkish stores and the surrounding countryside. Railroad and telegraph services were restored and new currency was printed and issued. "A thousand and one things had to be thought of," a British officer said afterward, "but never once was Lawrence at a loss."

On the following morning, October 2nd, Lawrence was awakened with the news that the Algerian brothers had started a small revolution and were aiming at seizing power. This was a foolish move indeed in a city which held the cream of Lawrence's highly experienced and campaign-hardened desert warriors. Swift planning, even swifter movement and a barrage of heavy machine gun and rifle fire crushed the revolution before it had time to get properly started. Mohammed Said was flung into prison; Abd el Kader escaped and vanished.

Lawrence worked almost virtually nonstop for three days at restoring order and quiet to Damascus and to good effect. When General Allenby and Prince Feisal arrived on the third of October, he was able to hand over to them an ordered and settled city smoothly and efficiently run by a capable Arab government. General Allenby was impressed indeed by the great achievements of the Arabs in so brief a period of time. He immediately informed Feisal that he was prepared to recognize Arab rule over the entire area east of the Jordan from Damascus all the way south to Maan.

Lawrence, on the face of it, should have been delighted by this. It would have meant the achievement of his and Feisal's dream of Arab independence. But Lawrence felt no such great joy. He knew that Allenby, an honest man who meant what he said, was repeating what he had been told to say by the British government. Whether or not the British government meant what it said was another matter altogether. But Lawrence made no mention of this to either Allenby or Feisal.

He now approached Allenby with the first and only personal request he had ever made—that he should be given leave and sent home to England. Allenby was most reluctant to grant this, as he wished Lawrence to push right north to the Turkish border. But Lawrence knew that his main task in Arabia was done, and he was in no mood to chase northward after the broken rabble of the Turkish army. All that could be done to achieve Arabian independence, he had already done. If there were any more he could do in the future, he knew it would not be accomplished by driving north on camel-back over the now conquered desert. Instead it would be worked out around the council tables of postwar Europe.

Besides, no man ever stood in greater need of rest. For two years now, forever short of sleep, forever short of food, his body racked by unnumbered bullet wounds, he had been the relentless driving spirit behind the whole Arab Revolt. He had covered tens of thousands of miles by camel, horse, plane and armored car. And in all that time he had never once thought or sought to spare himself. But now his goal had been reached and he was mentally, spiritually and physically exhausted—thin, wasted and burned out. Rest he was desperately in need of, and rest he must have.

Allenby recognized Lawrence's great need. Apart from the fact that he was a kindly man, he knew he could never refuse such a request from the man to whom above all he, Allenby, owed the most sweeping victories of his life.

Permission to depart was granted almost at once. The following day, after a last farewell to Feisal, Auda, Nasir, the Emir of Ruwalla and all his old comrades in arms, Lawrence left Damascus.

He arrived back in England on November 11, 1918, a fitting enough day for the return to his homeland. For at eleven o'clock that morning the last gun on the Western Front fell silent and World War I was finally over.

CHAPTER 11

A PEACEFUL SETTLEMENT

AND THEN, AS HAS HAPPENED TIME AND AGAIN throughout history, came the war after the war. This secondary war, like all the others before it, was fought not on the bloodstained battlefields but in the ordered peace and quiet of the international conference rooms. There the leaders of the victorious nations sat down to consider how the fruits of victory should be shared among them. There was no blood spilled around those conference tables. But national feelings and tempers ran every bit as high as they had during the fiercest moments of the war.

At the far from aptly named Peace Conference at Versailles, the temper of Lawrence of Arabia ran as high as that of any man present. Certainly it ran far higher than most. He was there as adviser, spokesman and interpreter for Feisal and the Arab nation. And with the passing of every moment in the conference chamber, he could more clearly see what was happening. The promises of Arabian independence and the setting up of an Arab kingdom in Syria—promises which he had made to Hussein and Feisal on behalf of the British government—were in the gravest danger of never being fulfilled.

At one stage in the conference, when he saw how badly things were going for the Arab cause, Lawrence proposed an alternative to complete Arab independence. He suggested that the French, as their share of the eastern spoils of war, should have the Lebanon and the northern coast of Syria. Meanwhile Feisal should rule from Damascus as the king of a smaller independent Syrian state. But the French would have none of this. Syria, they said, had been an area of French influence since the time of the Crusades; and they intended to have Syria for themselves. The French brought forward a very power-

ful argument to back up their claims. Britain, they said—
and it was true—was determined to retain control over
much of Mesopotamia (modern Iraq). As long as the
British did this there was no reason why the French
should not control Syria.

It is not difficult to understand the French attitude.
They had suffered terrible losses during the war with
Germany, far more than any other of the Allied nations. If
ever a nation was entitled to some sort of compensation, it
was surely France. Lawrence could see their point of view,
but what weighed with him most of all was the
memory of the promises he had made to Feisal. The Arabs
had fought their war for national independence; already it
seemed that the dreams were going to turn to dust.

Not that Lawrence was without powerful supporters.
Lloyd George, the great British prime minister of the time,
clearly saw the force of Lawrence's arguments. He had
strong sympathy for the plight of the unfortunate Arabs.
For his part, he would gladly have renounced all claim to
Mesopotamia, had the French been willing to do the same
in Syria. But, because of the peculiar political situation at
the time, part of Mesopotamia came under the control of

the government of India. And they were not prepared to give up the area promised to them. In addition, Western oil interests had designs upon Mesopotamia.

The Americans, too, were strongly on the side of the Arabs. American members of a commission sent to investigate the situation in the Near East strongly recommended that the French should renounce all claim on Syria. But the French remained immovable. Syria, they said, was theirs, and that was all there was to it.

To such a state did matters eventually come at the Peace Conference that Lawrence was prepared to fight and lead the Arabian army, if necessary, against both the French and the British. The British, it may be said, were no more popular with the Arabs than the French were. Not only did they still hang on to Mesopotamia; they were intending to introduce self-government for Palestine. And the Arabs feared the Jews might take still more land away from them.

Lawrence, however, was not required to fight against his own country and its allies. A rather unsatisfactory plan was worked out whereby Feisal was to rule a part of Syria from Damascus, but under French control. Lawrence had no faith in the permanence of this agreement. The French, he knew, were having serious trouble in the Near East. They were in a state of undeclared war with the Turks, who had not yet been demobilized. Revolutionaries in Syria were taking advantage of France's situation to stir up trouble. And the only man who could keep the country in order was Feisal. It suited the French very well indeed to have Feisal rule from Damascus—for the moment.

The uneasy truce between Feisal and the French did not last long. In March, 1920, an Arab Congress meeting in Damascus proclaimed Feisal as the absolute king of Syria. This rather rash move provoked the French into extending their mandate over Syria. "Mandate" is a very useful word which can mean many different things. In this case it seemed to mean that the French, in spite of their earlier agreement, intended to take over Syria for themselves.

Feisal, anxious to preserve peace at all costs, offered to meet almost any conditions the French wanted, but the French would have none of it. They advanced on Damascus, ruthlessly crushing all armed opposition, took the capital by force and drove Feisal off the throne. Many of the desert chieftains who had fought so splendidly by Lawrence's side died in the brief struggle.

This must have been the most bitter moment of Lawrence's life. All his and Feisal's dreams of Arabian independence, all their ambitions to give the Arabs their own home, all the splendid promises Lawrence had made to Feisal—they had all come to nothing, and less than nothing. The long bitter deadly struggle in the desert had turned out to be no more than a useless mockery. The Bedouins who had died had died for an empty dream. True, the Turkish overlords had gone; but, in Syria at least, new overlords, the French, had moved in to take their place. Everything was lost; the war had been fought in vain.

But, as is so often the case, the darkest hour came before the dawn. Lawrence's greatest work and his greatest achievement for the Arabs were yet to come.

At the beginning of 1921, the Near East was boiling over. There was trouble, and bad trouble, everywhere. In Egypt, there was a rebellion against the British. On the Palestine border the Arabs were at the Jews' throats. Open revolt broke out in Iraq, as Mesopotamia was now called. And, far to the south of Damascus, the Emir Abdullah, Feisal's younger brother, was threatening to get Feisal's throne back for him—if necessary by force.

In Britain, wiser and cooler heads clearly realized that there was one cause and one cause only for this widespread trouble. It was the discontent and anger felt by the Arabs who had been promised a nation or nationality and a freedom that had never come. Those same wiser heads knew that something must be done and done immediately before an all-out war flamed across the width of the Arab-speaking lands.

And so the government chose as colonial secretary the man they thought most capable of dealing with the situation—Winston Churchill. And Churchill, in his turn, picked for his staff one of the men *he* thought most capable of dealing with the difficulty. He sent for Lawrence of Arabia, and asked for his help.

Lawrence was delighted. He agreed to go to Cairo with Churchill, on the condition that Britain would honor, as far as it lay within her power, the promises he had given to Feisal of Arabian independence.

The condition was granted. There followed a whole

year of intense work. Churchill, Lawrence and the other advisers worked unceasingly, both in Britain and in the East, to achieve a satisfactory answer to the problem. And in the end they did achieve at least a partial answer, a plan to which Lawrence made a great contribution.

The French had by this time taken over complete control of Syria and no hope lay there. But Lawrence managed to achieve for his friend Feisal something even greater than the throne of that country. He secured for him the throne of Iraq, a land twice the size of Syria, with a greater population and far more promise of developing into a prosperous country than Syria had. Before this happened, of course, Churchill and Lawrence had to persuade both the British and Indian governments to withdraw their claims to Iraq. Reluctantly both governments eventually did this for the sake of peace in the East.

Feisal was freely elected king by an overwhelming majority of his subjects-to-be in Iraq and rode into Baghdad in triumph, at last a king with his own kingdom. Almost at the same time, and as part of the same master scheme devised by Churchill with Lawrence and his other advisers, Feisal's elder brother, Abdullah, became the ruler of Trans-Jordan (now Jordan).

And so, in the end, Lawrence must have been happier than he had ever thought possible only a short year before. His crusader's dream of freeing the Arabs from foreign rule had come true, at least in part. His own country, Britain, had come out of the agreement with head higher and hands cleaner, and he himself had been able to honor the promises he had made to the Arabs. His good friends Feisal and Abdullah were securely on their thrones. His long years of bitter hardship and endless suffering in the desert had not been in vain.

Colonel T. E. Lawrence was to live for another fourteen years before he met his death in May, 1935, in a high-speed motorcycle crash. But our story of Lawrence of Arabia ends on July 4, 1922. On that day, at the age of 33, he resigned from the Colonial Office, his task completed and his duty done.

AFTERWORD

WHILE LAWRENCE'S EFFORTS HELPED ACHIEVE
Arab independence from European and Turkish rule, the
Middle East has continued to this day to be an unstable
and violent place. King Feisal ruled Iraq as a constitu-
tional monarch until his death in 1934. The monarchy
ended for good in a revolution in 1958, when Faisal's
grandson, King Feisal II was executed along with the rest
of the royal family.

Abdullah, installed as King of Jordan, also met a violent
end. In 1951, he was assassinated by a lone assailant in front
of a mosque, as Abdullah was about to enter. His son, Talal,
became king for just a year and abdicated for health reasons
to his son Hussein, who reigned until his death in 1999.

Abdullah and Feisal's father, Hussein, the great Sherif of Hejaz, fared no better. After his family had ruled the Hejaz for a thousand years, he was defeated in 1925 by Ibn Saud, the ruler of the Nejd. King Saud had united most of the Arabian Peninsula, which became what is now called the Kingdom of Saudi Arabia.

Ironically, Auda Abu Tayeh, the most fearsome of all the Arabs who fought with Lawrence, retired to his home town of El Jefer, where he built a palace using Turkish prisoner labor! Unfortunately he didn't have a long retirement, as his many years of hard riding and fighting finally caught up with him. He died in his home in 1924.

At various times during the 1950's and 1960's attempts were made by leaders in Iraq, Egypt, Jordan, and Syria to unite as a single Arab nation, but due to the famous independent streak ingrained in the Arab personality, nothing came of those efforts. In fact, the Middle East has suffered from numerous uprisings, wars, and violent revolutions since the end of World War I right up to the present day.

THE EDITORS

Index

ABOUT THE AUTHOR

ALISTAIR MACLEAN is the best-selling author of a number of exciting adventure thrillers, many of which were made into feature films. Born in Scotland, he joined the Royal Navy when he was seventeen and served during World War II as a torpedo man on a number of ships escorting convoys across the Atlantic. After the war, he became a schoolteacher in his native Scotland. Always interested in writing, he entered a short story in a contest and won first prize!

Encouraged by that success, he drew from his navy experience and wrote his first novel, *HMS Ulysses*, about a navy convoy escort ship. It is considered one of the classic naval war novels and quickly became a best seller.

Books that have been made into films include Guns of Navarone and Ice Station Zebra and Where Eagles Dare. His books have sold millions of copies over the years and many of them are still in print. Mr. MacLean died in 1987.